BUYER-BASED MARKETING

WIDENING THE NET OF ACCOUNT-BASED MARKETING

MATTHEW KRASKA

Buyer-Based Marketing

Widening the Net of Account-Based Marketing Programs

www.buyerbased.com

Copyright © 2019 by Matthew Kraska

All rights reserved.

No part of this book may be reproduced in any form or by any electronic or mechanical means, including information storage and retrieval systems, without written permission from the author, except for the use of brief quotations in a book review.

Although the author has made every effort to ensure that the information in this book was correct at press time, the author does not assume and hereby disclaims any liability to any party for any loss, damage, or disruption caused by errors or omissions, whether such errors or omissions result from negligence, accident, or any other cause.

Version: Release 1.0

To DG, EA, and MH
Somehow, the three of you have motivated me to write this book. Thank you.

Jim and Joe
Thank you for all of your help.

CONTENTS

Introduction   vii

1. Program Output   1
2. Market Sizing   8
3. Providing Targets   20
4. Competitors   25
5. Competitor Products   32
6. Your Company   40
7. The Brand   50
8. Our Products   62
9. Classifying Customers   72
10. Buyer Profiling   83
11. Value Propositions   99
12. Code System   113
13. Content Marketing   120
14. Creating Content   134
15. The Webinar   150
16. Content Distribution   156
17. Failure and Success   166
18. Marketing This Book   179
19. This Book - Market Sizing   181
20. This Book - Competitor Analysis   185
21. This Book - Product Definition   192
22. This Book - Customer Boxing   198
23. This Book - Buyer Profiles   202
24. This Book - Content Marketing   212
25. This Book - Distributing the Content   217

Afterword   223
About the Author   227

INTRODUCTION

I want to make sure that everyone who reads *Buyer-Based Marketing* understands exactly what this book is all about. It is about marketing business-to-business services, manufactured products to businesses, and distribution marketing for large companies. I have devoted my entire career to perfecting this approach to marketing and will provide a number of supporting examples along the way. Now, to make an additional point clear: This book may give you some useful pointers for selling shoes to an 8-year-old, but that is not my intention. If you want advice on how to get your beaded necklaces listed on Etsy, I won't be able to assist you. What I can provide, however, is a system and a framework to make your marketing process better regardless of what you're selling.

I will provide a set of tools along with diagrams,

Introduction

process maps, flow charts, and templates. Work through those resources for your business, and by the end of this book you'll know more about your markets, more about your customers, more about your competition, and more about your own business.

The buyer-based marketing system contains many different pieces, and it is up to you to decide how or if you will use each one. If I had to wager a guess, I would think that most people would skip the market assessment piece, and that's ok. If I can defend it a little bit, it's essential to understand where you play, what the market is worth, and who else is in there with you. Don't skimp out! Plus, because it's rare to walk into a business and have someone explain how much their business could be worth with evidence to back up the statement, you'll look like a rock star. My best advice is to work through the entire system at least once, and then decide which parts you want to use and which you will throw away.

At the end of *Buyer-Based Marketing* I will outline the entire marketing plan for this book itself. I will self-fund all advertising and will demonstrate how to spend a little bit of money and track it all. I'm putting my own money where my mouth is, and if you're reading this, I've already proved that it works—one way or another.

Introduction

The Basics of the System

Buyer-based marketing is meant to be a framework of ideas and tactics that lead you on a clear road to profitable growth. If you're familiar with LEAN and the Toyota Way (TPS: Toyota Production System) this system follows a similar set of principles though it's not nearly as detailed and not nearly as reliant on people. This system takes groups of tactics and lays them out in clusters in an order of when I believe they should be rolled out. I provide examples of how I complete the tasks and align them to a strategy, but that doesn't mean that you can't use them in a different order or for different goals. Even if you acquire a nugget of useful information you've already won a small victory. Although this system will help you align tactics to a strategy, it is not intended as a strategic framework because this is a tactical framework suited for any number of different approaches.

Each component of the system is a piece of a larger puzzle, and when you put the pieces together, you'll have a complete solution set for any type of customer, in any served market, and for any of your products or services. You will be able to mix and match your pieces to create effective pitch decks, content for distribution, or even create marketing materials to support a distributor. I believe this is one-size-fits-all approach suits most types of systems, and it hasn't disappointed me yet.

Introduction

Many of the topics I cover in this book also live on my website, and although they're not in any sort of complete form, they serve to help you go further with the system. If you're looking for further explanation or need to see a diagram, chances are that I have it up on the site—and it's all free to access whether or not you have bought this book. I just want it up there as a supplement to this material.

Chapter 1

PROGRAM OUTPUT

Explaining the Output of the Program

I'm going to present an example of a program layout before we go into the details of the system. This list, along with the accompanying swimlane diagram on the website, is the basis of the program, but they are meant to be changed around depending on the specific needs of your application. This is not a "do it this way every time" scenario generator but rather a guideline and example of something that will be completed. I'll present the list and diagram, and then I will go into a little detail on each section, along with the corresponding part of the book where we address the "how": The most critical aspect of these programs is to understand the why first, and the how second. You will need to be able to adapt these ideas to fit your specific needs.

Program Creation

Buyer-based marketing is a rinse-reuse-recycle marketing system. You can create one program, test it, edit, and then reuse. You can use one program to cut the time needed to develop another. You keep building and building until you have a system of high-performing programs that almost run themselves. It's a long and laborious process to get there, but if you follow the outline below, and fully complete the sections, you will gain a deep understanding of your customers, the markets you serve, and where your product or service lives in a world of competitors. The best part is that you will have a precise and tested system to rely on—and one that you can use over and over again.

Size the Market

I include this step in every buyer-based process because buyer-based marketing itself is a collection of single programs, aimed at a specific buyer, in a particular market, for one specific purpose or set of products. Using a bottom-up approach that starts with individual companies is a compelling way to gather a large amount of information that can then be applied as valuable research material for a variety of different topics and tactics.

Analyze Competitors

Analyze the competitors to gain a better understanding of your place in the market and to know which of your general competitors are real competitors in this specific place. We break down how to understand what the marketplace looks like from a consumer/buyer perspective so we know if we fit in the way we think we do.

Analyze Competitor Products

Thoroughly understand competitor products, find pricing, and evaluate your position relative to the other products on the market that are targeted at the same vertical and to the same buyers. Improve your knowledge of the world around you at a granular level to play on your strengths and address hesitations.

Create Company Profile

Create a complete profile of your own business, from the point of view of a customer. Honesty without emotion provides messaging and decision-making benefits to the whole organization. I reuse my company profiles a lot, but because I include it in every buyer-based project, I keep it fresh and updated. Things change, and going through this exercise every time may get repetitive, but it also makes sure you're putting your best foot forward.

Define Brand Assets

Not every buyer-based program will contain branded assets in the sense of a product, but this will give you the opportunity to reflect on the need for a specific brand (if recognition of a particular product warrants a brand) or if your competitors are using a brand for a similar product/service. For the instances where you do have a product brand name, you need to continually evaluate what the brand means to a prospective customer, and what it is that you say the brand stands for; these are often very different things.

Define Your Products or Services

This is the definition of your product from an industry and buyer perspective. These include cost, function, and value, although not necessarily cost-based value. We also work on creating a product-based value proposition as an independent entity.

Customer Boxing

Here we will use a customer-stratification system to gain a deep understanding of what it is we sell, to whom, and why they might be buying it. Learn how to segment customers into different groups so you can easily alter plans to attract more of your most valuable types of customers. Continue to group customers to gather useful data that can help guide your decision making processes.

Buyer Profiles

Creating a buyer profile is the final key component of building a plan and understanding who it is you're targeting. You will put together all of the pieces up to this point to create a real program to target actual people right in your sweet spot.

Final Value Proposition

In this section we cover the importance of the final value proposition, a statement directed at a specific buyer, in a specific vertical, with a variety of potential products. This statement is what you'll spend money promoting, monitoring, and adjusting.

Data Collect, Test, or Position

Here we talk about creating the value-added content that will be used as the meat and potatoes to push our final value proposition. How do you get a buy-in from the people you need to create this content? How do you plan around it? How do you get to the finish line with something that provides value to a prospect?

Content Marketing

In this section, we wrap the creation portion into the context of what content marketing is for buyer-based marketing: how you can roll out information to prospects and current customers alike to increase revenue from a variety of sources, including pull-through, perception alteration, brand recognition, and other avenues.

Distributing the Message

You're almost to home plate here, where we discuss how to distribute the message. This is not a comprehensive list of marketing channels but rather a mating of different systems that have worked for me, and what I believe are still the most effective channels of value-based messaging propositions.

A/B Testing

Finally, we get to A/B testing: the act of monitoring and refining your message to ensure that over time you create a lasting effect on customers. This is where you take away the odds of creating the perfect proposition right out of the gate—and if it doesn't, you should be prepared to understand why it doesn't occur.

The Output and Its Ability to Change

I go into a lot of detail in this book, and some readers might think that I over-explain some things. I do this intentionally so as to make sure that all my readers are on the same page, as it were. Now, it's true that you don't need to use every part of this system or use each element in its entirety to see some benefit. Some of you might want to skip right to the product definition and start from there. That's fine. Others, however, might begin with market sizing and stop before you ever get to the value-proposition stuff. It's also possible that some of you may scoff at the use of a coding system, which I recommend as a way to keep track of what it is that you're doing. It's fine if you don't want to use this system, but I discuss this only to explain how *I* use the system and why I use each part as I do. As long as you get something from this book it's a win for me—and for you.

Chapter 2
MARKET SIZING

Market Sizing

Total addressable market, serviceable obtainable market, wallet share, whatever you want to call it, this part of marketing is one of the hardest to understand with confidence. Too often companies will run with the mentality that if they create a product people will buy it without taking the time to understand what the market looks like. Understanding what the market size is, along with the potential for growth within that market, can help empower these decisions with intelligence. Proper market sizing is useful, practical, and once you get the hang of it, it's not that hard.

The below explanations are based on my experience. This type of approach is not the same across all types of businesses and is much more straightforward for companies who know the pricing and have some sales data on their competitors. For the rest of us, the challenge here is vast and undefined.

I don't think you'll find any one particular way to approach market sizing, but you will find two different types of analysis: top-down and bottom-up. I'll stay away from textbook definitions, and to keep it simple we'll say that top-down is when you look at the total size of a market—say, U.S. pharma sales (about $450bn in 2016)—and then apply some simple math to figure out what your potential share of the market is. For a bottom-up analysis, we start with what we know about the market and build from that information to create our own view of the possibility. The way that you will calculate the market size in a button-up analysis will differ greatly depending on what type of product or service you're selling. Even though a market sizing exercise can be difficult, when you have some information about your current customers, you'll get a much more accurate number than if you rely on a report you purchase over the Internet, which in my experience have always been drastically wrong.

A bottom-up approach is when you start with what you know and apply it on a smaller, company-by-company scale. Let's take a closer look at that pharma sales number I cited a moment ago. We know a few other things about our example company for the sake of this explanation: the company sells an item that goes inside the pill bottle to help preserve freshness, the price for this item is $0.06. It doesn't go in every pill bottle, but it goes in many. Instead of using the entire pharma industry number (we'll get back to that later) we're going to select a sample size of companies, ensuring that we choose some that we currently do business with.

You'll need to make a few assumptions to build your data model of information. For this example, we will look at the companies we do business with and find their yearly revenue (Hoovers, Crunchbase, or a quick Google search). First, let's estimate the volume percentage that we believe we need to see our wallet share. If we think we have 100% of available business with a customer, we'll make a note of that. If the company is taking in about $500m in yearly gross revenue, and we sold them $150,000 worth of product (assuming we have all available business), we can assume that like companies convert at about .03% (.0003 if you follow my math). We would apply the .03% to the gross revenue of all the companies in our market sample to come up with an addressable market. It's not always this simple, but this should be the mentality you take into the next section where we discuss identifying what you need to know and how to organize the information to give you a realistic number.

A quick note about market sizing: **Make it a habit to record what you and your company know about the market. You'll have to talk to sales people and other legacy company employees (you may discover that all of the information you need is typically stored away in their heads).

Making the Information Useful

We will begin by outlining a spreadsheet for all the information. I use an Excel sheet because each market that we monitor may follow a different column layout, and more complicated applications will require a weight column to adjust some numbers. Baseline columns include Company Name, Type, Applications (a color-coded column), Company Revenue, Revenue Adjustment (20%), Average Product Price (at source), Our Product Cost, Gross Adjustable, Obtainable (Potential), and Current Share.

This spreadsheet gets much more accessible to fill out if you currently do business with a company, and as a consequence you'll find that most of the hard math is simple to figure out. If you have a business that matches your identified market, and you know how much of their potential inbound volume is consumed, you can apply that formula to other companies that you don't do business with. This is also where the output and possible market opportunity gets a little dicey. The more businesses you work with, the better your assumption of the volume is—and the more accurate your opportunity value will be. If I'm in a hurry, I take that adjusted percentage from each company (same math as above, but with a company where you have a dual-source agreement, it may end up being closer to .00015) and come up with an average. I can then apply that average to the entire sample size. The larger your sample size, the closer you'll get to the real market size number.

The less information you have, the less accurate your projection of available market will be, but at least you'll have an explanation to go along with the number you provide or use. At its most straightforward I like to use a company's total revenue metric and initially adjust the amount down from 10%–40%. The value is adjusted down to account for revenue that may be coming from streams other than what you see as core products. I tend to apply a more significant percentage of adjustment to private companies, as the revenue estimation provided by websites like Hoovers or Crunchbase tend to be inflated. We then need to perform another few calculations, but first, we'll talk about gathering some other information that you will use to complete the spreadsheet.

You will need to do your best to make an educated guess about what the available market (at a per-company level) looks like for your particular product offering. A company like General Dynamics has many different divisions, departments, and businesses. If you look up the market cap and divide by two, you'll get pretty close to their yearly revenue (or if you have access, look up their annual revenue). If you're selling a component that only fits into a Gulfstream G500 business jet, you would need to figure out what portion of their business, revenue-wise, is from that jet. For a public company, this can be pretty easy; for private companies, it's another story. Use whatever intelligence gathering methods you have and make sure you include the knowledge of the salespeople that you have at your disposal. They know a lot about your competitors and the companies that you're trying to sell to. For now, we'll assume that you're on your own and you will have to do all of the research in a vacuum.

Step-by-Step Process for Selling a Product to a Business That Sells to a Consumer

To get started on the "how" of this process, we're going to assume that you have an existing business. We'll list the steps and explain them along the way. Make sure that some of your current customers are included in this spreadsheet. This step-by-step process is an illustration of selling a manufactured part to another business that will then sell to a consumer (public company).

Open the spreadsheet that you've created with the columns listed earlier in this chapter.

1. Create a list of companies. Find a company in that industry/market and group by SIC (Standard Industrial Classification), NAICS (The North American Industry Classification System), or a combination. I like to use SIC here because it's always been more manageable for me. Because your market size might include many products and companies that span more than one product type, there will likely be many different SIC codes that apply. I group these codes and give my code number (explained later). I then use all of those SIC/NAICS codes to find other similar companies. I double-check them to make sure that they apply to the products that we sell. It would be best if you aimed to end up with a list of about 50–100 companies.

2. Look up the company's yearly revenue and put it in an additional column.

3. Create a classification system for the vertical and try to apply as many to the sheet as possible. In the case of a pet food company, I would have a column for each of the following: Kibble, Dry Treats, Meat Snacks, and I would put an X or color the cell for each that applies to that company. If you want to get more detailed, you can look up how much of their business is in each segment and use a weight to determine their revenue on the pieces that you play within. Instead of an X or a color, you would put a total number (as revenue) per section, and then apply a percentage weight to it.

4. Create a weight column to implement a standard deduction from the gross revenue number. I usually use about 25% to be conservative and account for miscellaneous revenue that doesn't apply to my sizing.

5. Create a column for the average estimated price.

Here is where you need to be smart and do a little research. For a company that makes pet food, you would look at how much their average sale price is for each segment and combine it after the segment columns.

6. Create a unit count column. In this column, you will divide the final adjusted revenue number (either the combination of your segment columns or the column in which you add up the multiples) with the cost per unit average to get a unit count.

7. Create a column for your average unit price.

8. Create an obtainable column. Multiply your unit price by the number of output units.

9. Create a current share (Units) column; if you currently sell to this customer, put in how many units you've shipped in the past 12 months.

10. Create a current share (Dollars) column; if you currently sell to this customer, put in how much money you have in shipped goods or services over the past 12 months.

Now you're at the point where you have to check your math and apply some common sense to your formulas. Double-check all of the end math with the customers who already buy from you to see if it passes your smell test. If you know you are dual-sourced with a customer and have 33% of the business, you already know what the available market value is for that specific customer. Get your formulas to line up with what you already know.

You can also do this in a somewhat reverse format to come up with a multiplier for a gross revenue number. If you have ample customers where you know you have 100% of the business or 50% of the market, you can apply a common multiplier (say, if you consistently show up as 0.03% of gross revenue in your 100% companies) to everyone in the industry and skip a lot of the guesswork.

Some things to consider while filling out this spreadsheet:

- What percentage of products in their core group of offerings do you serve?
- In the case of a large pharmaceutical company, your application may only factor into the packaging of one or two drug lines, how big are those drug lines?
- How much of their current applicable business do you serve?

Step-by-Step Method for Selling Software to a Business with a Limited Number of Users

This process is very similar to the B2B example above, but some key differences exist, such as the fact that we care more about the number of users within a company and not how much product they will buy from us for use in their product.

1. Find a company in that industry/market and group by SIC, NAICS, or a combination. I like to use SIC here because it's always been more manageable for me. Because your market size might include many products and companies that span more than one product type, there will likely be many different SIC codes that apply. I then group these codes and give my code number (explained later). I then use all of those SIC/NAICS codes to find other similar companies. I double-check them to make sure that they apply to the products that we sell. It would be best if you aimed to end up with a list of about 50–100 companies. If you can sell into any market, this base list of 50–100 units can be multiplied by the total number of businesses in the segment.

2. I look at the number of employees in the company and write that down.

3. Now we have to apply some tricky math to get the possible employee count that would use the product. We'll say, for this exercise, that we sell software to finance departments. In many manufacturing companies between 0.015% and 0.018% of the employed personnel of that company work in a finance capacity. We would add a column in to apply formulas to the total number of employees within a company. I usually do this by performing a Google search on the number of workers in any specific category. Some have data by the census bureau, others you have to guess by asking around. You'll first want to know how many finance people work at their company, then take an average, and then you'll be further along than you were before.

4. I now create a column for my average monthly license cost per user (what is each person work to you).

5. I multiply column three with four and get my available number.

Many people think that they can easily size an entire market from your product's perspective, but I don't think it's really ever that easy. In the above example, we are selling a software product, and you could say that it applies to every finance person out there, and you could very quickly size the whole market from a total user perspective. I don't do this because I attach my market sizing to specific buyer-based programs, and each market will have different needs and get a different value proposition. I keep my market sizing as granular as possible every time, so that I know more about the people that I'm going after.

Between these two examples, you can see how the same basic system can be used to figure out how much money is out there for you. Likewise, hopefully, you will start to think a little bit outside of the box when you try to size something.

Applying a Code to the Market Size

This is the first code piece we will apply to our program. This isn't code in the sense of programming language, but a code that enables us to quickly identify a complex series of actions through time and will track ROI a little bit better than any different type of naming convention. I'll explain how this is used later in the book. For now, add a code to the title of your document or in your reference materials when talking about this market.

For market sizing, I code the most granular information available; whatever sub-market I have researched gets a code. If I have the food and beverage industry as a top level, I will research each component that fits my product or service. As an example "canning and bottling companies" would get a market report and a code of M-1, and "snack food co-packer" would get a market report of M-2. The number you apply here is important only to the extent where you can tie everything back to a market report so that everyone can understand what you're talking about.

Chapter 3
PROVIDING TARGETS

Bonus: Providing Targets for the Sales Team

While you're sizing the market, you can begin to collect information about your targets. Because the market-sizing exercises in this book rely on a granular approach for building the basis for market size (company-specific rolled up into a total), you're already most of the way to figuring out who exactly you need to be targeting.

Although I usually group market sizing and targeting into the same exercise, you don't have to. For some buyer-based programs you might decide to complete this section after you create a buyer profile. I find it helps me to create my target title list here while doing the market-sizing steps.

You can approach this in many different ways, and

there are a ton of various tools available to help you complete this. I only use two, and it seems to produce results pretty quickly. When you finish the market-sizing portion of your process, you will have identified a group of companies by SIC and NAICS codes.

I use my market-sizing spreadsheet and create a new tab/sheet and list out all of the companies in a column. I leave four or five rows for each company so I can put names, email addresses, and phone numbers in the columns of the sheet.

Tools That I Regularly Use

Tool 1: LinkedIn Sales Navigator

I use LinkedIn Sales Navigator to figure out who is who in a company. Later on, in the Buyer Profile chapter of this book, I talk about defining target titles, and I use LI Sales Navigator for that as well. I don't believe that you need to go through the Buyer Profile exercise before you start to write down your targets for salespeople, but it might help depending on your circumstances.

I start by running through my Hoovers list grouped by SIC/NAICS and search for the company on Sales Navigator.

I scroll through all of the people that I find and try to pick out titles that I think apply to my target list. If

I'm selling an engineered component, then I would look for people in R&D. If my product is much cheaper than my competitors, I will look for people in the purchasing department.

I put each name in the spreadsheet in an open row for that company, and I repeat this process down the company list (or I have someone that I trust to do that for me).

Tool 2: Hunter.io

After you have gotten all of your names filled in you will need to do a little bit more research. I like hunter.io the best out of all similar options for finding an email address. When you put in a company website address, it will scour the Internet for every mention of an email for that company. This will give you the name of the email for that company.

- f.last@whatever.com
- first.last@whatever.com
- flast@whatever.com

Under the company name, I will place the email address (you'll have extra rows under the company name to do this). After this is completed, you can run through the list of names and put in the email addresses. I usually run this through an email-address validator as well before I hand it off to sales. I'd also like to point out that it would be terrible of you to go through all of this work only to then put these email addresses into an automated drip campaign. If you want a better chance to win, write them a real, personalized email.

Other Additions to the Spreadsheet

Depending on how important this is to my current project, I also try to include the target person's location. If I want to send direct mail or engage them through phone calls or whatever, I want to know where they are. If you're targeting a large company that has many locations, you'll want to know that Bob Bobberton is in Washington D.C. Then you can look up his address and corporate phone number. If a salesperson wants to initiate a call, they can call the phone number that you've provided and ask for Bob Bobberton. This type of information is helpful to a salesperson. It can also help you schedule pop-in visits or whatever other shenanigans salespeople do these days. Along with all of that, I try to include whenever possible the following information on a per-person basis:

- Location listed in Sales Navigator
- Closest corporate location to that person's listed location
- Nearest corporate location's front desk telephone number

More Information

I call this chapter a bonus because none of this information is vital to the buyer-based process, but it can be of great help to the sales team. This type of target list is becoming more useful as many sales teams are shifting focus to the inside such that email drip campaigns are becoming less effective. More things are done online than in the past, and sales teams tend to be more reactive (at least from what I've witnessed). I always complete these tasks or have my team complete them when we go through this process. You're already in these pieces of software and you've already got the spreadsheet, so why not?

Chapter 4
COMPETITORS

Competitor Analysis

The fabled SWOT (Strengths, Weaknesses, Opportunities, and Threats) analysis: It's useful to a point but how many times has someone pulled out a SWOT and made a decision? There isn't enough there. I'm not telling you that they are garbage; I just find such analysis to be limited in the real world. Instead, I like to lay out a competitor analysis in a chart (not too dissimilar to a SWOT), with the aim of providing actionable intelligence. I'll say this a lot throughout this book, but you will need to rely on your salespeople to complete or to help you with some of this work, but the benefit is that when you get finished with these competitor charts, you shouldn't have to keep asking the same questions.

The following fields are always included in my competitor analysis:

- Primary Facilities/Locations
- Estimated Sales of Competing Products
- Markets Served
- Top Customers
- Primary Applications
- Solutions Offered
- Value Propositions
- Highlights

Primary Facilities

Primary facilities are listed to give a geographic background of competitors. This is important in distribution and manufacturing models mainly, as logistics can play a significant role in pricing and speed of delivery. In the Internet age, the location of a business or their support facilities is far less critical than it was in the 1970s, '80s, and '90s. When I research the topic of geography concerning sales volume and competition, most of the solid stuff comes from those year ranges. I do believe that logistics capability and cost still comes into play for many manufacturing companies because they are generally creating a large number of somewhat cheap items that are used to progressively add value to another person's products—right up until they get to the consumer. This is where geography becomes important, from logistics to the cost of freight. The location of a competing facility is certainly helpful to know.

Location also remains important outside of manufacturing. For example, if you provide call service for business finance, it would be important to know if your competitors use international call support. It's a good idea to capture the location during this stage instead of skipping it and having someone ask the question later. Plus, you might find something out that you didn't know before.

Estimated Sales of Competing Products

Estimated sales of competing products are when you take products sold by a company that competes with yours and estimate the sales volume. For instance, if you compete with a large conglomerate that produces many products, you're only concerned with the business unit or division that creates the products of concern. This program revolves around creating a large number of niche information points. For this we want to start at the product level.

Markets Served

Markets served is where we store information about the verticals and sub-industries where this competitor has market share. For instance, GE occupies many markets, including Logistics, Finance, Aviation (engines), Healthcare, and many more. This can help you gain insight into where this company might be going and if your competing products are part of their core strategy or just happenstance.

Top Customers

Top customers is a list of their largest customers that also purchase products that compete with yours. This can help you drive targeting, and help you come up with a plan to take market share. You might not always know this information completely, but as long as you're not new (and this book is not for startups in entirety, although some of it is applicable) you should have some information on whom you have lost deals to and who else controls market space. If you don't know any of this information, you need to look at why your salespeople don't know anything about their business.

Most decent sales organizations have a lot of in-the-head information about who controls what market space. If you deal with large numbers of customers, it may be harder to ascertain precisely who controls what share, but you should be able to make a reasonably educated guess with the help of the people around you. The idea here is to get better over time. Once you get everything written down in one place and people have the chance to review it and know how to look out for these things, you'll see that the quality of information you have gets better and better.

Primary Applications

The primary application is a list of applications their products or services target. This is meant to be a little bit more detailed than the markets they serve, and different than the solutions they offer. This is the application base of their product or service. For example, if you're providing a call-out service for sales teams, your competitor's applications might be "sales support for software-as-a-service," or if you sell blister packaging to the EU healthcare market, your competitor primary applications might be "blister packaging foil enclosures." This is meant to segment the competitors by application of your product. How are customers using your competitor products?

Solutions Offered

Solutions offered is how their product would be categorized. If you're competing with a radar systems manufacturer, they may only sell radar solutions, or they may be developing Light Detection and Ranging (LIDAR) equipment also. This is not the same as the application portion, and this list accounts for directly competing products or services that they provide. It might not be a 100% direct match, and, hopefully, they aren't a direct match. This is about identifying products that a consumer (in the B2B sense) sees as a possibility of choice. Each product that your competitor offers that might compete with you should be listed here. You can use this list to begin your competitor product analysis, which we talk about later in this chapter.

Value Propositions

Value propositions are useful to record on competitive analysis, and it will give you insight into how that company sees itself, and how you may adjust your strategy to correctly separate yourself from the market's perceived notion of the competitor. You can get these from collateral you have collected from a trade show, from a website, or from a newsletter that they advertise in. I like to make sure that every time a competitor directly references a product or service that I record how they talk about it.

Highlights

Highlights are just a note section and may be used to put down thoughts about the company. XYZ is partnered with Mitsubishi to ease logistics flow in and out of Japan. Any information that might be important to you that isn't contained above can be put here for safekeeping. I normally use this section to capture logistics information, but depending on your circumstances you could use it to capture anything, from general notes all the way to pricing guesses.

Learning About Your Competitors

The good thing about being thorough with a competitor analysis is that the document becomes living, and this particular portion of the information you collect won't change too much. Every buyer-based strategy launch can reuse this information, and the value here is that you get to put your message into the context of these competitors.

When I address competitor analysis, I like to look at what they're presenting and how they present it. When you roll out these programs, you learn a lot about the industry, and what you think is working may not be working. I don't talk much about addressing their position in marketing channels, and although it can be useful to monitor, I generally don't include it in any formal matrix. I also don't add it here because of the amount of work it can take to track marketing in trade publications and through newsletters. If I can, I'll follow it when I find it, but I don't actively seek it out.

Chapter 5
COMPETITOR PRODUCTS

Competing Product Analysis

Just as much as you need to understand your competitors, you need to understand their products. The fields here change a lot depending on what it is that you're selling or offering, but they can give you clarity when it comes time to develop your value propositions—and you'll make better decisions in the process of avoiding a "me too" mentality. This is also a little different than the analysis of your own products because you won't have as much reliable information available, and your interpretation of their brand, messaging, and imagery may be different from someone else looking at the same material; nonetheless, the importance of understanding and documenting competing products shouldn't be understated.

I would also like to take this time to point out that you should keep this information—such as price points and what you believe their cost is—in some type of spreadsheet so you can graph the data later. All of this quantifiable information is best presented to stakeholders in a chart format.

The fields I use to capture this information are similar to our product definition:

- Value proposition for the product as a whole
- List of benefits
- List of weaknesses
- List of most useful features
- Unique Selling Points (USP)
- Cost (if known)
- Price (or a close estimation if not available)

Most of these will be educated guesses or taken from web resources and field research, but the idea is to gather a complete picture of these products from the view of the person who would be buying them. In other words, put yourself in your own customer's shoes.

Value Proposition for the Product as a Whole

I put this first for competitors because you're not the one using the other information recorded to build the value proposition. This should be the main statement about the product or service and should be readily available. In some cases, they won't have a value proposition, or at least you won't be able to identify what it is. That's better for you, as they probably aren't as focused on explaining the provided value of their product. If this is the case, just put down "none" in your record. If you come across one later, put it in.

Benefits

Look at all of the available information from websites or literature and write down all of their listed benefits. If they have a bullet list of benefits, take the whole thing; it doesn't matter if you believe it or you have some bias against your competitor. Take their word just like a prospect or customer does because the goal is to learn from their marketing messaging. If all of your competitors are addressing the same set of problems, they are on to something, or they are showing you a gap in their benefits. This comes into play a little later when you craft your statements and start to understand your current customer mix. If you see your customers complaining about the same things, and none of your competitors are addressing them, you've uncovered a weakness.

You'll be served well if you approach this task with neutrality, and instead of taking the side of your own company, take the point of view of the consumer and assume that most people will believe what they read when they are looking for a product or service—as long as the statement isn't way out there. Benefits are also different than features (I'm going to remind you of this a lot because it's very easy to confuse them). The benefit is what a feature—a part of the product or an approach to service—provides for you. A benefit is what that feature or approach does to solve your problem.

Weaknesses

These can be a little more opinionated than the benefits or value propositions. This is your take on what these competing products are not offering, or what their marketing messaging is not addressing. These are your targets for differentiation. If you know your customers' need-on-time delivery because they manufacture consumer-facing goods that rely on your product and no one is talking about their logistics capability, you've found a weakness.

A weakness may go beyond messaging or marketing, and it may go into the product itself. If you've bought your competitor's product, and you notice some flaw in function, some unpalatable imagery, or anything else, now is the time to write it down. I always like to look at and test these products. If you have an R&D lab you can use to run tests on the products, do so to find out how their products are different than your own. Figure out how much difference there is in the performance, acceptance, or function between your products and their products.

Whenever I can, I like to run tests on our products and our competition's products. I make R&D people angry sometimes, but the benefit of doing this type of testing cannot be overstated. I cover this a little later in the book.

Most Useful Features

Record what you believe are the product's most valuable features; there may be more than just a few here. Is there a handle design that feels better in your hand? Does their packaging lend to the function of the product? Anything that you would classify as a feature of a product or service should be recorded here. It's not a benefit but a stated aspect or element of the topic.

Feature Benefit Statement

A feature of a Nest Learning Thermostat is that it is Internet-connected. A benefit of a Nest Leaning Thermostat is that you can control the temperature of your home while you're at work.

Unique Selling Points (USP)

What is the unique selling point or points of these products? This will also be a mix of marketing messaging and actual in-hand product testing. Once you start to fill out more and more sheets you will probably have a realization: Many of these unique selling points are not unique at all. That's the point of including these here, and you will catch selling points that are common across the industry that you fail to capture. Maybe some are important, and perhaps some are not.

Cost

The cost section is going to be left blank for many competitor products. One of the hardest challenges you can face in external business intelligence is figuring out the cost of competing products. This is what it costs that company to make this product. You might be able to make a good educated guess, or your salespeople might have worked at a competing company before, but you should at least try to capture what information you can about the cost. By far, this will be the most unreliable metric used in this book—and I never base any decisions off of this information. I keep it solely to keep track of what I know and what I don't know.

Price (or a close estimation if not available)

If you're familiar with distribution margins in your industry, you can look up prices through a distributor and take away their cut (average known distributor margins). Many manufacturers will use a distribution partner or partners to supply orders that cost them too much to service themselves. For example, if it costs you $300 to fulfill an order, taking it from order entry to collecting payment and shipping, you would likely (hopefully) not accept a request for $280. The distributor can service the trivial many for a fraction of the cost, but they need a margin.

I cover customer boxing later in the book, but it should be mentioned here that service drain customers should always be moved to a distributor.

Back to the point, learn the typical distributor margin in your industry, look up pricing, and then discount that margin. Now you have a reasonable cost from the manufacturer.

Using Competitor Products and Services for Information

Whenever I start a new gig or begin working with a new company, I learn as much as I can about its products or services, and I do this by gaining a thorough understanding of what the competitors are doing. Most companies are not very honest with themselves about their products and services, and believe they're already the best, the cheapest, or whatever and "we just need more marketing." Going through these exercises to fully understand your competition, on a product-by-product basis, will allow you to be more honest with yourself and your company.

Chapter 6
YOUR COMPANY

Company Definition

After I complete competitor analysis, competitor product analysis, and market sizing, I move on to an internal investigation of a company's strengths, its core principles, and the value of the products that are sold. I do this for every buyer-based program that I create. I might not recreate the entire definition every time, but I at least give it a once-over to make sure that nothing has changed and to refresh my memory of the core principles that drive the organization.

Company Strength and Position

Determine the classification of the products or services that are sold. Are they low cost? High quality? Brand dependent? Ask yourself questions about what it is that defines your company.

I'm going to use a fictitious scenario of a motto and brand assets. Let's assume that the established company statement (currently used as a value proposition) is: "We provide technical solutions for marine industries." We are not a low-cost provider of a product, and the cost is generally the same or slightly higher than most competitors. I also know that part of the value proposition is that the products are manufactured in the United States, often carry hard-to-get certifications, contain ultra-high quality components, and are supported by the company throughout the lifecycle of both the product being delivered and the customer's final product.

That group of sentences gives an idea of their position in the marketplace, and it lets you know that you can't move much on price, but you need to ensure that you're conveying that message to customers through the website, collateral, sales strategy, email, and every other possible way. You need to make sure that the customer is aware of your position in the marketplace. High-visibility brands are not shy about charging a little more for their products. The quality might not even be any higher than low-cost competitors, but you might be paying for prestige, or the expectation of excellent customer service. I know this sounds like what you might read in every other marketing book, but it's important to keep your goal in mind.

For company position documents I like to define it just like product awareness and very similar to a buyer profile. This exercise makes sure that everyone in the company has the opportunity to comment on and is agreement with the core offerings and the language used to describe them. Core business statements, whether they are vision or mission statements, are important to disseminate throughout the organization. Both internal and external acceptance is important, and the people relaying the message are just as important as the people receiving them. It's not always about putting those types of statements throughout your message. It's about making sure that people are aware that your goal is what it is. For many companies, this branding move ensures that the core message is consistent, and the customers with whom we do business are aware of our position and intent.

Company Position Worksheet

I like to keep this information in a spreadsheet as well because it will let everyone see and come to an agreement on the language used to describe the company. I like to use the following fields:

- Company name
- Company value proposition
- Company core functionality (sandbox)
- Company mission statement
- Company vision
- Company key products by volume
- Company's key brand assets

Company Value Proposition

Creating a value proposition is a lot like getting your teeth yanked out of your head by a donkey with legs the size of toothpicks. It will take him forever but he won't give up, and it will hurt like hell. No one will like it, right up until you hit the perfect one. Value propositions are a large part of this program, and their importance cannot be overlooked. Please don't skip this section because you think that your value prop is as perfect as it can be. The worst part about this for businesses that have many different targets for many various projects is that you should be providing different value propositions to different targets, for different products. That can be a lot of work. A whole chapter of this book deals with the final value proposition: the one directly marketed to prospects, but I also want to cover each value proposition along the way.

There are many different thoughts on how to create a value prop, and some outstanding ones range from three to four words, and that seems to work very well in the software industry. What happens though when you're a manufacturer of air filters? It's a jam-packed market, and it's just an air filter. That's the problem that you need to solve with a value proposition: If your air filter is fundamentally the same as everyone else's, it must provide some value beyond the surface application of filtering air. If it's the cheapest air filter out there, your value proposition writes itself: "An air filter that cleans air like an air filter should, for 20% less." You'll sell many air filters. If your air filter is more expensive, why is it more expensive? Having a lousy manufacturing process isn't an excuse that most people will want to hear, so you need to have something else to catch them with. I know this sounds like common sense, but it's not because I've seen it happen in all but one of the companies that I've worked for.

This is where value additions come into play. Think value because everything that you do should be about providing value to the customer. What is the value that you're going to offer with your expensive air filter? To do this, I like to make a bullet point list of all the different values that my filter provides, all the value that my company offers in the context of the air filter, and any additional value that is provided by the team that is behind the filter.

For the company's value proposition, you need to tie all of the things that you do and wrap it into one small display of value. Later on we'll go into the structure and how to create the value proposition, but for now you should be creating a bullet point of all the company-wide value statements. Examples of company-wide statements:

- Ten-year limited warranty on every product
- Free service for five years
- 24/7 customer service
- Engineering services to support manufacturing processes

Company Core Functionality (sandbox)

I like to define this on a worksheet so that everyone involved understands what the business is all about. Very often, and particularly in smaller companies, this gets muddled with "the next big thing." This can backfire spectacularly in a manner akin to Kodak not wanting to cannibalize their film business and give away digital photography technology. Core functionality is a definition of where the company plays, and you'll have to get used to saying something like "we need to find a partner to do this for us." Every company needs partners, and whether they are distributors, film extruders, logistics, and supply chain firms, or anything else, they are and will be important for you to achieve a core function. Understand what it is that you really do and do well. Focus on those things first.

Company Mission Statement

I'm afraid to tell you that this book is not going to teach you how to create a mission statement. I've never been in a position where I was required to produce one. If you don't have one you should think about creating one, even if you don't have the authority you can bring the topic up. Chances are your company has some type of mission statement, but I've never put much stock in advertising a mission statement. However, for some companies it does show up in presentations and other forms of informative documentation, so I suppose it can be useful.

Company Vision

A vision statement follows many of the same principles of the mission statement, but it is often more forward-looking. This also appears in many of the same places; however, it is much more common to find vision statements penetrate the marketing realm. Many huge companies and organizations use their vision statements as marketing tools. That's fine, but we won't be using it very much in our buyer-based processes. Still, its relevant to put it down here so you have a complete picture of what you're doing.

Company Key Products by Volume

For this you will need some access to data, if your ERP is hooked up to your CRM, you're in luck. If you are part of a small or medium-sized business you might have some trouble convincing the finance department that this type of information is needed in marketing. However, it is. I know that different companies run with different mentalities, but this data is part of the marketing realm. If your company isn't being honest with their employees you probably need to ask why.

The reason we need to put this information together is to understand better what our reality is, and where you want to spend your time. Do you think you have a product that is growing a lot because all the salespeople can't stop talking about it? Get the facts before you make a big decision to spend time or money on it.

Later on, we'll talk about customer boxing and how that handles half of this issue (key products by volume). This can be a more significant discussion all by itself though, and some of what will occur when you start to understand your product mix is the issue of what you want to make, what you need to make, and what you want to get rid of if you offer many different products. Knowing what volumes you have and what that customer mix looks like will help you make marketing decisions based on fact, instead of guessing.

Company's Key Brand Assets

The chapter following this one is all about your brand assets, and although I don't claim to be the best brand guy out there, we'll touch on some simple methods to make sure your brand is clear and consistent when being presented to a person. An excellent start to that chapter, and whether or not you use that portion of the system, is listing your brand assets here. Do you have any products that carry a registration mark? Do you trademark any of your brands? Anything that is recognizable as a product or service name should be listed here so that when you go through the exercises in the next chapter, you'll already have somewhere to start.

Continuous Improvement of Your Definitions

I like to make sure that I keep this part of my buyer-based programs as updated as possible, making sure that you're moving your marketing mix along with the priorities of the company. Mission and vision statements don't usually change much, and the frequency of additions or deletions to your brand assets is just as uncommon within established businesses. Core functionality and key products are likely to change often though, with the latter being susceptible to geography, season, and myriad other factors. Keeping an eye on these ebbs and flows of business can help you make more informed decisions in the right spot and at the right time. As a rule of thumb, you should also look over and update your company definition with each new buyer-based program implementation. You probably won't change a lot, but if you follow that guideline, you'll always have something up to date to provide to salespeople, your marketing team, or the executive team.

Chapter 7
THE BRAND

Brand Assets

Emphasis should be put on organizing and maintaining a file of brand assets, if for nothing else other than for registration purposes because when your trademarks and registrations come due, it's better if you have a living document to prove they exist.

For buyer-based marketing though, you need to periodically review your brand assets, the messaging used to communicate brand value to customers, and your position in the marketplace. We talk about some of this in the product definition section, but keep in mind that a brand might encompass more than one type of product.

I create my list just the same as every other

spreadsheet list that we cover in this book, with fields to fill in:

- Brand name
- Locations of use
- Budget allotment
- Importance to the company
- Notice in marketplace
- Value of brand

Brand Name

This is pretty simple. On the spreadsheet or whatever you're using, put in the brand name.

Locations of Use

This isn't location based on geography, but rather on an area of pure marketing distribution. You need to know how many times your brand is used throughout your collateral, website, and any other place where a person who is interested in your product might come across the brand name. As you start to define your brand names (think any time something is trademarked, service marked, or registered) you need to know how important they are to your company.

Understanding this and putting it down in writing helps everyone understand what your position is. You can start to determine if your brand value is worth the time that you spend maintaining them, or if something has immense brand value such that you might not spend enough time or money on promoting it.

You will need to monitor, record, and display every place where a brand name is used, and you need to codify that just like everything else. I will cover a lot of this later in the book, but for now, let's suffice it to say that I call all of my brand items B-#. If I have a brand name of ABC, in my code structure I use B-abc or babc. It becomes essential to know when you start spending money and understand buyer profiles and the market worth of your branded products. When I create a pay-per-click (PPC) ad or a piece of sponsored content, I always use URLs that contain my entire code structure (by using www.whatever.com/product?a1-b2-brabc). This allows me to directly track every action made by every buyer, for every product, for each brand, and in each market.

Performing this action, particularly if you're moving into a new company that has never had a real marketing department, is vitally important. This will make you look like a rock star, and you'll be able to prove the value of a brand identity. If you have no brands associated with products, and you're over $5M a year in annual revenue, you might want to consider the possible value of branding some of your products or services. It doesn't matter if you sell common widgets that go into a toilet or if you make parts for

Rolls Royce. Consider brand names beyond your company name.

Budget Allotment

After you complete the above step, it's important to understand what the budget layout is for any specific brand. This step and the steps below are interchangeable in terms of when you complete them, but the importance of assigning a dollar number to a brand cannot be overshadowed. You can't just run never-ending PPC ads to try to elevate a brand image. It would be best if you started to understand, from a budget perspective, how much on a percentage basis you are willing to spend to distribute your messaging per brand, per product, per buyer, and everything else.

Importance to Company

I like to use a scale of 1–10 for this section. Certain brands bring in more money than others do, and in most cases, for a B2B business that is under $50–$75M you never really understand what the true market position is. If you use Salesforce, this job is a little bit easier for you (if your enterprise resource planning—ERP—is feeding data), as you can segment by product groups and figure out what product position is. I don't want to get too far down that rabbit hole in this book. However, you will need to begin compiling information on what product groups fall into what brand, and then rank them based on importance. It would help if you involved your salespeople to take on the role of information gatherer here—and to use no bias in your ranking.

This importance ranking will help you look at what has resonated in the industries served, what might have worked well in the past from a product and messaging standpoint, and what might work again in the future. This will also show you which brand names have been devalued internally or externally. If a core customer product has become devalued, part of your job to fix it or trash it. To fix it, you will need to know what the problem is first.

Notice in Marketplace

I also use a 1–10 scale for this, and it's a little easier to figure out than the importance to the company section. If you're selling Air Jordan's, you can assume that you know exactly how important that brand is to the company—and pay a ton of money for the licensing deal. For the rest of us, we don't know how well known we are unless we begin to capture the information. Collaborative efforts smooth out the information gathering process here, and you should always include as many stakeholders as possible. What you can't get caught up in is the belief that your company is already the most well-known and highest-quality provider around. This is the internal self-indulgence that occurs everywhere: "We're the best." It's never true. There is always someone out there that does something better than you do. It's how they make money.

To accomplish this in an unbiased way, I like to begin with the salespeople and customer service to ask about how often they use our brand name in communications, or if they relate direct product information. I then try to figure out how important the brand is to us internally. I then ask questions about how often the customer uses our brand name and how familiar they are with our internal language. If they're familiar with our internal language, I tend to lean toward a high level of brand importance.

The Questions I Ask for an Internal Brand Survey

- How much time do we spend internally with this brand? (This could include R&D, marketing, sales, etc.)
- Does the company rely on the brand to survive?
- What would happen if we killed the brand and focused on advertising our value prop? (Or is the brand our value prop?)
- Do we believe that prospects understand our brand?
- Do we think that current customers understand our brand?

I then use the Internet to search for our brand terms, look through distributor listings to find out if they use our brand terms, and I put together an aggregate score. This score is not strictly defined, but rather a rolling scale with our worst brand pulling a 1 and our best pulling a 10. I don't think any hard-and-fast range here would do any good for anyone. You're not trying to build a new metacritic site for your products, but you will want a snapshot of sentiment.

Value of Brand

In this section, I don't mean the dollar value of the brand, and unless you're someone like Nike, you probably have no way of knowing exactly what a specific brand is worth. I mean this in the sense that this gives every stakeholder clear access to where a particular brand is on the spectrum of importance. This is important when we start to talk about ROI of advertising, and if you begin to track this now, you can establish a baseline of what is valuable to your company and what is just a waste of time.

I use the "Notice in marketplace" score and the "Importance to company" score to figure out this number. I use a 1–10 scale for this number too, and it should never be an average of the two components mentioned above. This should be a gut feeling that grows in accuracy over time. It would help if you determined which brand names, images, and messaging are the most important to the continued success of the company. This will help you make budget arguments, or help in any discussion whether or not you continue to use a brand name to define your products. If you are a "me too" type of producer, using a brand name might diminish the potential value of the product. You would spend more time advertising "ABC Mattress" than you would for advertising "Memory Foam Mattress" and thereby give a value proposition for something that people already buy.

Making Your Brand a Real Part of Your Program

Let's say, as an example, that we recently launched a new product, and it happens to be the fifth iteration of a current project and is an evolutionary leap forward in terms of aesthetics, function, and cost. We went through the process of product definition described in a different chapter of this book and then needed to land on a brand theme. We have many competitors that play in the ultra-low-cost spectrum, and many of their products work, albeit not nearly as well. We have a few real advantages: Ours is manufactured in the United States (target customers are all in the United States), our formulation is more consistent and has better benchmarks, our company employs lean manufacturing processes (so our customers can depend on our logistics), and we offer lifecycle support and equipment. When we went to market, we needed to put ourselves in the shoes of the customer, who happens to operate on razor-thin margins: "What's in it for me?" We needed to encapsulate our brand and message around that question.

We decided to brand our product as BrandX, created a great looking logo, and set off to define what that product brand was. All of our material, reports, and other documents both internal and external were heavily branded. In our marketing materials, we went to the customers with a clear definition of what BrandX is, how it's different, and what's in it for them. The core principle is to establish and reiterate, over and over, what BrandX is to them and what they get out of helping us change over to the new product. Life isn't simple for anyone, and any time you have a new product or change an existing product, you need to understand how that affects the customer (provide value by thinking about them). Your brand assets need to align, from a messaging perspective, with your company messaging.

We performed some studies on the efficacy of the new iteration and presented them along with new quotes to our existing customers. We made sure that our BrandX logo was on everything:

- BrandX logo on reports that were professionally printed
- BrandX logo on all quotations
- BrandX logo and statement on value proposition sheets
- BrandX logo on salespeople clothing
- BrandX logo on all materials presented to the customer
- BrandX logo on website and blog articles

We took every step to ensure that each time we refer to our product we use the term BrandX. I can show you how this works because you've seen BrandX a few times by now (it's not the actual brand name that was used by the way) and I would bet you anything it's already well stuck in your head.

A Story for Your Brand

We also made sure that we came up with a good story for the brand. In this case, the product is not a new product but is instead a rebrand attached to a few changes in the product. Developing this story and making sure it's everywhere we talk about the brand is essential as well. We need to come up with a value proposition for the brand as a whole, and then explain it a little more. We need to answer this customer question before they get the chance to ask it: "What's in it for me?" They will then begin to remember what your value proposition is and attach it to your brand name automatically. We all do this all the time with the brands we buy. You can do this too, even with your widget. If your world is a world filled with widgets, then you know about widgets. If one widget has a high value attached to it and you recognize the brand, you're more likely to buy that widget than one that you have no experience with.

For a Consumer to Understand, You Need to Understand

You have to be more intimate with your brand and its assets than any person who does not work for your company. If someone else knows something about your brand that you don't, how can you expect to win? From sales numbers to specific use cases, once you start to wrap your arms around what your brands are worth and what the potential for expansion is you can make better decisions. For me, an essential part of outlining the brands that I influence is the realization that many branded products are just commodities with no real value associated with the brand specifically. Understanding the brand from a form, function, and market perspective equips you with better tools.

Chapter 8
OUR PRODUCTS

Defining Our Product or Service

You need to be aware of your product strengths and weaknesses. Every single company I have ever worked for gets caught up in the thought that they're doing it better, that their products are inherently great, and that people around the world purchase them because they know that the products are the best. This is never true. Ever.

Just like a buyer profile, you will need to profile your products, and like everything else in this book doing so will make your job of creating and distributing valuable content to specific people easier. If you're not getting it yet, this whole system is just like college, and you'll get out of it exactly what you put into it, nothing more and certainly nothing less. For product profiles I even like to follow a similar model to everything else:

- List of most useful features
- List of benefits
- List of weaknesses
- Unique selling points (USP)
- Value proposition for the product as a whole

Once you start going through this process with your products, it will help you to understand your position in the marketplace better, and it will significantly aid in the speed at which you can create content. The whole idea behind the system is to tackle one piece at a time but to do it thoroughly. That way when you need to write something or come up with a pitch deck for Product A, for Customer B, for Market A, you can pull the pieces together. If you need to then pitch Product B to the same customer and market, you can pull that together relatively quickly as well.

I use a custom application from Zoho Creator to keep everything in check, and a few years ago I taught myself Ruby on Rails and built an entire application that handles an earlier version of this program. But what I learned was that in reality it was just as easy to keep everything in a spreadsheet. Depending on how large your team is, this can be unwieldy, but it is a smaller initial effort. Because individual components are so highly customized, like market sizing and content dissemination, it's pretty hard to make a one-size-fits-all solution.

Creating the Sheet

I create a spreadsheet (an example is available on the resources section of the website) and list products by row and make sure I leave enough space throughout the sheet to accommodate four of each category except for the value proposition (you only need one of those).

Most Useful Features

I usually list features before benefits, as they should each have a corresponding benefit or group of benefits. A list of the most useful features is similar to benefits, but benefits are what a feature does, and features are what a product or service has. A list of features may look like:

- Integrates with any EMR (electronic medical record system)
- Works on any device with a web version and a standalone app
- A clean and easy to use interface
- Integrated, secure, message transmission for records and images

Benefit

I list the most important benefits that I can think of. A benefit is not a feature; instead, it is a purpose for the product or service, what problems does it solve, or what were the ideas behind the design.

If you're selling a referral management system for hospitals, your list might look something like:

- Reduces the time required for an initial patient visit
- Produces a clear view of referral channels and their value
- An increase of the Hospital Consumer Assessment of Healthcare Providers and Systems (HCAPS) scores by increasing patient satisfaction in processes
- Enables referral communication with patient and care providers

Benefits on the product level are all of the benefits that apply to that product. These will be split off later, where a buyer profile will focus on a few specific benefits. I like to keep as many as possible in this list and spend some real time here because it will make my life easier to come back to this spot and pull them into other positions. I also try to match up every listed feature with at least one benefit. If you can't think of a benefit for a feature, you should be asking yourself if it's really a feature at all.

Weakness

I am then completely honest with myself about the weaknesses of the product:

- Small support staff
- Does not allow for auto-deletion of un-encrypted stored images
- Does not integrate with medical record collection agency software
- Is a startup

The importance of being honest and understanding your faults will allow you to prepare better sales and marketing messaging for the buyer hesitations discussed elsewhere in this book. The "is a startup" bullet is a perfect example of this basic honesty. If you're selling software in the hospital space, you need to understand that they are generally slow to adopt and many find it hard to trust a startup. Lives are at risk, their margins are important, and existing systems most likely work well enough. If you ask them to replace their current referral management system or processes, you need to understand that they may find it difficult to trust that you will be in business for the next five years.

You can counter this argument by ensuring that you're funded for years, have a strong customer base, or are willing to sell the system as a stand-alone self-hosted solution that doesn't rely on you staying in business (albeit worded differently than that).

Unique Selling Points (USP)

Unique selling points are the features, benefits, or attributes that make your product or service unique in the industry. These will be used with everything else in the list to create a single value proposition for the product itself.

- Modular software that is sufficiently extensible to fit the needs of an organization
- A hierarchy for users and managers allows account-level-control throughout an entire organization
- Referral marketing network built into the system
- Full physician referral listings with merged rating and comment system (from all available online sources)

You might see some crossover between your USPs and your features and benefits, and that's ok. The point of this particular spot is to clarify what sets you apart.

The chances are that you share many features with many competitors, and many of your benefits will be shared with many of those same competitors. This is where you focus on what makes you unique. Not unique like you have an abnormally short finger or that you have two different color eyes. Neither of those is unique. Truly unique stuff would be like saying if you're the only person in the world with two different eye colors and an arm that never grew. Focus on that stuff.

Value Proposition

Creating a value proposition is never easy, and I go into this in depth elsewhere in the book, so I won't duplicate my efforts too much here. The system relies on value propositions at every level of the marketing program. Buyers have value propositions that target them. Specifically, products have value propositions that are for the product, and markets have a value proposition that targets the market as a whole. The product value proposition is one of the two (along with buyer profile value prop) that will be used heavily for inbound marketing.

A straightforward example of a value proposition for the above product could look something like this:

Hospitals and health systems now have clarity into patient referral pipelines and care-provider networks with an EMR agnostic, fully supported, referral management system.

It's not perfect, but it hits some significant points that are important for the product. You would never address all 12 bullets above, but you need to pick the important ones to include, and then use the remainder in any other content that you distribute. The value proposition you create here, along with the product information is used for final value propositions in any account-based marketing programs.

The value proposition on a product level would be used on the website, in catalogs, or in the case that you sell a single product to a vast customer base. The systems used to develop a good value proposition are all pretty much the same but can follow a different set of rules for format depending on how you want to separate them. You will use all of the bullet lists from above to begin crafting your value proposition, so keep them handy for later.

Applying a Code Structure to the Product

The code for the product lives a little bit like a consultant, and it's used by everything else in the system but doesn't necessarily use the other parts of the system. The structure follows the same pattern, and I call mine PRO-1, PRO-2, and so on. The code is vital on the product level because it can show us how successful a campaign or set of messages is based on the product being sold. In some extremes, you'll find marketing people who say the product doesn't matter and that it's about selling a belief. When you're dealing with B2B customers, the product most certainly is important. More than half of that organization that you're trying to sell to only cares about the product and its price. In many cases they hardly care that it works; it might just be a checkbox on a form that they fill out. For that reason, I put a lot of emphasis on always selling a product to a buyer, not selling a buyer on a story. That statement might sound like a contradiction or a cop-out, but it's not. You still sell a product to a buyer through a value proposition. My point is that you're not selling a "story" to many buyers, you're selling a product.

Product Definitions to Create Content

This effort is usually rewarded with self-creating content, not in the sense that your content will all of a sudden materialize like it's been transported to you from the starship Discovery, but rather the process of creating product-based content is pretty simple. You'll have a clear list of everything that's good, bad, value-driven, or otherwise a sticking point. You can use this bullet list to create the messaging that is used to describe what it is your product or service does.

Going through this section thoroughly will reward you with untold rewards later on. At the very least, and even if you stopped here, you'd be better off understanding precisely what it is that you're selling. One of the pleasant side effects of being honest here is that you will be much better equipped to deal with any buyer hesitations (identified later) from a product or service perspective.

Chapter 9

CLASSIFYING CUSTOMERS

Customer Boxing

Existing customer stratification (boxing) is not necessarily a fundamental component of a buyer-based marketing system, but bear with me through this one. I call my system customer boxing, which is similar but simpler than the aforementioned customer stratification system. With this system you can begin to understand the questions that your core customers ask, what commonality exists between those you want to work with and those you don't. Once you go through this process, you'll begin to understand that you have a treasure trove of information about what messaging works, what's vital to your valuable customers, and what their common pain points are. You'll walk away knowing more about what type of messaging to use.

It may not be the most methodical approach, but a simplified four-box system will help you get up and running quickly with customer stratification. Dr. Barry Lawrence, and John Mansfield, of Graybar, have developed and provided a comprehensive approach to customer stratification at Proformative. Their methods dictate that you classify customers into four basic categories: Opportunistic Customers, Core Customers, Marginal Customers, and Service Drain Customers. In the available resources, I will provide a diagram that you can fill out to start classifying your customers. I slim down their system quite a bit, and remove many of the tactics required to truly stratify a customer. I don't spend any time understanding time-to-pay, returns, quote conversions, inventory levels, and suppliers of the customer. If you're interested in performing a deep dive into customer stratification, I suggest you check out Dr. Lawrence's material at Proformative's website. It's worth a look if you want to take this approach to the next level, but I don't want to steal any thunder there. Their material is worth a read.

I choose to take a simpler approach because I want to use it for marketing, to understand my customer mix, and to apply a messaging standard to get more of the customers I want. I also want to figure out what my key customers value in a business partnership.

The Four-Box System

This system of customer classification aims to define four moving metrics: margin dollars, customer attrition, sales volume, and cost to serve. We use these four metrics to categorize customers and begin to understand where and how we attract and serve customers in these categories. This methodology can also expose weaknesses in the rest of your business, and many of you may find that you don't even know what class of product you have, what is easy to make with good margins and what is not. In service-related industries, many companies take the "a dollar is better than nothing" model, where they will continue to work with annoying and low-profit customers without realizing they are taking time away from the core of the business. Below we will look at how to categorize your customers and assign a code to them so you can start directing your marketing programs to the right people and through the right channel.

Opportunistic Customers

Opportunistic customers have high margins, no sustained relationship, a low cost to serve, and a low volume. This means they buy a limited number of parts and provide a very favorable margin. They are not a strain on your corporate resources. To me, these are relatively rare in manufacturing. In some instances,

R&D heavy, customized products created just for a specific customer will force that customer into this category. Many military applications and customers end up being opportunistic. A customer ending up as opportunistic depends largely on what it is you are making or offering. If you look at Adobe Creative Cloud, for example, most of their customers are probably opportunistic. They buy one license that covers two computers, they don't ask many questions, and pay with a credit card. It's almost passive income to Adobe.

Core Customers

Core customers, at the top right of the box, have high loyalty, high margin, high sales volume, and a low cost to serve. These are the bread and butter customers of your business. You probably won't have very many of these, but they will also generally define the health of your business. Using Adobe again as an example, their core customers are likely made up of the top 10% of their enterprise accounts. They probably create relationships with these customers by providing regular service calls and are always available to handle any problems that arise. They treat these customers like they are special and will often include them in trials of new software or other activities that are reserved for only those that truly matter.

Marginal Customers

Marginal customers have low profitability, have no relationship with you, have a high cost to serve, and buy in low volume. These customers are in the bottom left of the four-box, low gross margin, and low sales volume. Using the same Adobe model, these would likely be the customers that purchase just single software licenses, like LightRoom. These customers don't have a high amount of loyalty, and if another solution comes along that does the same thing for much less money, they are likely to switch. They are low profit because they are only buying a single license to a single product. This is also why you've seen Adobe change its pricing model over the past few years in order to yield a more profitable business. They craft their messaging and pricing models to reflect the ideals and desires of their opportunistic and core customers. The marginal customers are lovely for revenue, but provide little value to the company as a whole.

Service-Drain Customers

Service-drain customers are low profit, have a high cost to serve, purchase in high volume, and also have a sustained relationship. These customers generally fall into the "business we'd like to avoid" category. Many reasons exist why we always have these customers and continue to do business with them. If these types of customers represent a significant portion of your revenue, you will have trouble getting rid of them unless your business has no problem making a mess of their income statements. Overall margin percentage might go up, but most companies are either measured by gross revenue or a combination of gross revenue and EBITDA, not just margin percentage. I'm not so sure Adobe has many of these customers, as I have never worked there. If we imagine that they do, these people would likely be legacy customers who purchased some enterprise agreement years ago and are immune from any pricing change initiated by Adobe. They may also have bought and continue to use such a large number of licenses—and Adobe doesn't want to lose the revenue even though margins are low and they require a ton of support.

Further Classifying the Output of the System

According to Dr. Lawrence, you would then further split these boxes into categories of business that we want to do, business that we have to do, and business that we don't want to do. These not only apply to customers but also may apply to good customers who buy products that we don't want to be making.

Business We Want to Do

The business that we want to do includes core customers, healthy products, either the product or customer has strong growth potential, and they have a low cost to serve. These are the customers who make our jobs easier, work with us, and buy the products that we like to make.

Business We Have to Do

This group of customers comes from service-drain customers, products that we don't mind making but aren't perfect, the economics of scale are at play, and they have a moderate-to-high cost to serve. Customers that fall into this category can be those who require a ton of customer service, need to audit you regularly, enforce their manufacturing practices on you, or place a large number of small orders. They tax your ability to serve your core customers effectively.

Business We Want to Avoid

These customers cause substantial aggravation, buy products we don't want to make, low economies of scale, and they have a high cost to serve. These are the nightmare customers whom you would dump right away if you weren't worried about the loss of revenue.

They're the customers who are probably better served through a distributor.

Boxing (Stratification) Output

The reason why this model, or one like it, is so essential to your marketing plans is that you need to start understanding what type of messaging attracts which kind of customer. Once you get smarter through the buyer-based process and build a useful data set, you'll also begin to understand what channels draw which type of customer. This is a fundamental building block of creating that becomes more effective programs over time.

Applying a Code to Customer Stratification Groups

We will get into the code system we apply to everything based on the categories of this book in detail later on. For now I will put this into context for customer boxing here.

You want to start by selecting a group of customers who buy similar or the same products that exist in the same market vertical. If you sell software-as-a-service to the banking industry, you're going to have an easy time because you have one product with one customer base. If you sell that same software into a few different verticals, we're in business. That's not to say that you don't do this exercise and classify your customers and code it. I'm just saying that it's easier to do the more limited you are.

Set some selection criteria for your first group of customers, and you won't need to be too specific about it for this first piece. We'll circle back later and redefine who is in this group. For the sake of getting ahead of myself here, I assign stratification groups as such:

- 1 = Opportunistic Customer
- 2 = Core Customer
- 3 = Marginal Customer
- 4 = Service Drain Customer

CB stands for customer box, and so the final code I apply for a core customer is "CB-1." Select your first group of customers in the core group. Make sure that the customers you select are all buying products in the "We want to make this" or "It's easy for us to service these" categories.

Once you have your first selected group of customers, go ahead and assign them code CB-2. You won't have real definitions for the verticals or their buyer profiles, but you don't necessarily need them yet. For now focus on understanding what these customers are. I keep all of this information in a spreadsheet or a custom app on Bubble or Zoho Creator. I think it's much easier to keep everything in a spreadsheet while you're still figuring out what it is you're doing and how you need to organize the information in a way that works for you. Every spreadsheet that I make has a column for a code. And I'll say this again here: I don't mean "code" that's going to be used to program anything; I mean code like something you'd whisper over a walkie-talkie. So this space on the spreadsheet starts with one code item (on the customer) and then expands to about three or four columns on the buyer profile.

My Plea to Not Skip Boxing

This part of the system might seem like an easy skip or a no thank you to many of you reading this book, but give me a few more minutes of your time to explain why you should consider what I'm about to say.

Even without any current customers, thinking about what will make up this list will help you direct your message and know before anyone buys anything from you where you should spend your time. If you're starting this process and you or the people around you haven't put any thought into this, how do you know you're treating your core customers right? How do you know when to fire a customer? You might know off the top of your head what a bad customer looks like, but have you put any real structure in place to define a bad customer? It might turn out that your lousy customer is a core customer and you need to do more to address their problems or concerns.

All I'm saying is that you think you know, but you probably don't know what fits into any particular category. Putting some structure around how you feel about your customers will help you focus your time, messaging, and value proposition to the right people. I have no customers for this book as I write it, but you'll see later on that I go through the exercise, so I know what to look for before it slaps me in the face. This will also help you keep track of the messaging, marketing channel, and the mix to attract more core customers and fewer of the service-drain type.

Chapter 10
BUYER PROFILING

Buyer Profiles

Buyer profiles (or persona, depending on who you listen to) are a way to classify a group of people you target with a specific type of messaging or through a particular channel. These become important in buyer-based marketing because they let us monitor the performance of language and tactics to a degree. If I want to target R&D employees of a hot dog company, I will tailor specific messaging to that person, and then engage in a targeted tactical campaign. I would want to understand their pain points, key drivers, economic concerns, and the industry outlook. I need to know if a trend away from pork hot dogs is occurring and make sure my product is aimed to help them solve their beef hot dog problems. For the purposes of this program I don't call these buyer personas because I want to focus on the tactical aspects of the targeting methodology. It's not about emotions, although those are very important parts of a buyer journey. However, this isn't a buyer-journey program. This is a program about targeting, tracking, and understanding the very top of the funnel.

A buyer profile is a coded number that represents organized information aimed at the top of the lead-generation funnel. I know in other systems time is spent on the motivations of a buyer and what they're feeling and thinking, but the aim of a buyer profile is to give you a real way to interact with targeted people inside of a classified system so that you can prepare yourself to do business with more of them in the future. I'm not telling you to throw away your persona or buyer-journey work if you've done it. I just find them somewhat irrelevant when you're producing materials in a real-world setting with limited resources. For emotion-based selling, buyer personas are a huge advantage, but in B2B I like to focus on my interpretations of tangible findings. Huge companies probably see benefit with these systems because they have the time and resources to make sense of it all, but if you're part of a small team (or solo), good luck to you.

From a real-world tactics standpoint, we need to trim down the exercise of creating these profiles to something that is meaningful and manageable.

The Key Factors of a Buyer Profile to Be Used in a Coded System Are as Follows:

- Primary Problem
- Secondary Problems
- Unique Selling Points
- Buyer Hesitations
- Key Features
- Key Benefits
- Value Proposition

This also goes without saying that you should name the profile—something like Director of Research and Development–Pet Food Brand Company—and attach a product or products to it, and assign it a market. The buyer profile is the last step in the process, so it should contain the most links to other components.

Buyer profiles also use the product listing that you completed earlier in the book. A product has a large number of features, benefits, unique selling points, and value propositions all their own. Now is the time to tie that information to a specific buyer. Cost is probably not a primary concern when you're targeting an engineer, but if you're trying to put messaging together to get past the buyer, you need to focus on price. A VP of operations is probably more concerned with the impact your product will have on their process than a VP of finance would be. All of your product information needs to be redirected toward the buyer, including the particular set of needs, wants, hesitations, and target features.

I use five elements in my buyer profiles instead of four because I like to make sure I have their potential hesitations in the mix. These are much different from the buyer persona information that you might already be familiar with. A buyer profile is used for something specific, and from what I can tell a buyer persona is used to understand what a particular person is thinking. I've yet to find someone who can clearly define what they are used for in B2B, and when you get to the point where you complete one and ask what's next, you usually have to sign up for some email automation software. No thanks. Let me get straight to the point on what I see as the main problem here.

Primary Problems

Many startup companies quickly develop products or software to solve a singular problem that they have noticed or experienced. Large- and medium-sized established organizations tend to believe that they already know exactly what the customer problem is. If you pay attention closely, your solution might solve some or most of a buyer's problem but probably not all of it. To get better at providing value to a customer, you have to think like that customer, and if you don't know where to start, try asking them. Most people will be happy to tell you how your product sucks, but they also may not want to fill out a survey, so you might need to get out of your comfort zone and pick up the phone.

If you have a sales team, they need to be directed to contact their customers and have a session where they discuss what we could be doing better, specifically about the products that they buy. If you don't have a sales team, you need to do this yourself. Call them (or ask customer service to ask on every call), figure out what their problems are, and how far off you are in solving their entire suite of issues that they expect you to address. Most people love to complain, and this type of call, in my experience, is generally much more informative and pleasant than a sales call. You're just trying to make your product better for them by providing more value.

The key here is to make sure you're writing it down in the buyer profile so you can start to track it. Write them all down, and my guess is that you'll start to see some commonality. As you write all of these issues down, you'll need to identify the most important one. I usually go through my entire list of topics and find the most common one that is the most difficult to address. I make that my primary problem.

Secondary Problems

Because you had already created a list of problems when you contacted your customers, this section is a little bit easier. Your job now is to determine which of these pain points are secondary to the primary problem for this buyer. Secondary issues should be placed into the appropriate category based on your belief in their merit and validity. You can only have one primary problem, but I would suggest that you put everything else into the secondary category so that you can keep track of what your customers think is important. When you write content or develop a new product, you can always refer back to this list and figure out if core customers and their associated buyers are having their questions answered.

Unique Selling Points

Unique selling points here are a little different than the USPs in the product section. These are the unique selling points of your entire organization, product, and services to this specific buyer. The selling points that you define here will drive a lot of the messaging that you will provide throughout the buyer-based marketing process.

It's important to understand the difference between a USP here and within a product; here these act more like mini-value propositions. You need to know how you're unique to this buyer specifically. The more adept you become at this process, the easier it becomes to morph existing buyer profiles to new ones, and many of them will have a great variety of overlapping similarities.

The USP attached to the buyer profile will become the foundation of your value proposition, and the aim should be that every bullet point you create here is included in every piece of material you can get in front of this buyer. I like to think of unique selling points at the buyer level as the same as every bullet you would read on the home page of a single buyer-targeted product. The list you make here should have a bullet of everything that you offer to this specific buyer that you believe is unique, or of rare significance.

Ensuring that you capture effective unique selling points will help you differentiate between insignificant and important. When you bullet these things out and start to put the pieces together, you will begin to see patterns that may have never been visible before. These are the critical aspects of the program that can't be overstated, and you need to understand what drives your core customers to begin to attract more of those.

Buyer Hesitations

This is my favorite topic in the entire buyer-based book, and it also happens to be the most overlooked section of information in many marketing programs. Here we try to figure out what hesitations any buyer has during any stage of their purchase process. It's not a simple task, and most people would assume that this category is limited to pricing. So I'll follow this up with a note about pricing.

I believe that any buyer hesitation can be answered by a good value proposition or statement of value from the company to the buyer. You need to figure out what it is that you offer that is different from the other competitors who are lower on cost. If you don't provide anything but a higher price, you should probably be asking yourself what you can do to stay in business.

Buyer hesitations exist in many forms. If it's a large organization that makes products or provides services, it becomes obvious that the company doesn't rely solely on one customer to support them. When you find yourself in this situation (and you should always act like you are in this situation) you need to figure out what hesitations exist that prevent them from purchasing more from you.

I like to list and record any hesitation that I'm aware of from a buyer, and I want to be as specific as possible. Because of the large number of potential hesitations, I will provide a small sample list below of what you might start with:

- The cost is high compared to competitors
- The product fails in our production line more than your competitors
- The service provided is not in our native language
- Your service department charges money to solve problems that are your fault
- Your customer service is not well connected to your sales team

Key Features

The key features associated with the buyer are a little bit different than anything that you have written for the company or your products. We look at key features for the buyer based on what the buyer finds most important. Key features (and their benefits) should align, in a perfect world, directly with the buyer's hesitations. We want to make sure that our products or services are precisely what the buyer wants, and if they aren't what they buyer wants, then we will find trouble when we try to sell them a product or service.

Here, I list out all of the key features as we see the product first. I move on to key features as the buyer sees them and then later merge the lists. Most people in the companies that I work for follow the same adage: We're the best, and we make the best stuff, and people will buy it because it's the best. This idea that you're the best, you know your real position in the market for a particular buyer, or whatever else you tell yourselves, isn't right. You need to understand the markets, your products, and the buyers before you can understand what these key features are.

You need to write down your honest key features: what your product provides to *this buyer* that is key. Maybe it's support, maybe it's the logistics behind your product, perhaps it's the interactivity of your software with theirs, whatever it is you need to document it and write it down. You need to be honest with yourself before you can be honest with a buyer/prospect/customer. This also includes talking to your salespeople and figuring out what is essential to the people they talk to. I like to create and enforce a questionnaire for each customer visit. If the company spends money on sending a salesperson to a customer, we need to get something out of it other than the creation of a relationship from the purchase of dinner and booze.

I typically include questions that need to be answered like:

- What concerns did they have?
- What complaints did they have?
- What did they say that was complimentary?
- In your opinion, how do we not properly serve this customer?

It doesn't have to be a long list, but you do need to

keep track of this, so the obligatory "this customer loves us" comment doesn't end up losing the customer in the future. This goes a little bit deeper than the topic of this book, but it serves a purpose here too: We need to know what our customers need and what the critical features of our product or service are.

Key Benefits

Benefits are different from features. Where a feature is something that your product has, a benefit is something that your product or service does for a person. For example, a coffee cup has a handle (feature), and the handle protects your hand from getting burnt (benefit).

You will need to list out these benefits, and I usually take them directly from the feature list. Because these things are fundamentally the same (they're just worded differently), every feature should have at least one benefit, and every benefit should correlate to at least one feature.

Your list of features might be something like:

- Easy integration with multiple APIs
- Simple user interface
- AI supported auto-complete logic

The benefits from those features might be something like:

- Connect all available APIs with the click of a button, without the need to understand programming
- Easy enough for anyone to use, with only four menu items and clear instructions your newest employee can start being productive right away
- AI-based logic takes away the guesswork from complicated math functions and analytics

I'm not the best benefit writer, but these will form the basis for many of your value propositions, and in some cases, you might find that your benefit statements can be combined to create a value proposition word for word. I've never been quite so lucky, but the worst-case scenario is that this will at least make your messaging line up.

Value Proposition

Just so we are both aware, I'm going to repeat myself a few times on the value proposition front, and I hope it sinks in that I don't have all the answers here—and I don't think any single person does. All I can do is give you advice on how to make something meaningful. The issue arises when you think about your product in the context of the buyer. This value proposition will be the most important one that you make. It will also depend on you completing all of the sections of this book before you get to this point. This is the final and most crucial component of your messaging. You need to look at all of the value propositions, hesitations, features, and everything else that you have defined earlier and come up with something that makes sense to this particular buyer profile. I usually call the buyer profile value proposition the final value proposition. It is the most specific and is used in all of my buyer-based campaigns.

The chapter immediately after this one describes the methodology that I use to craft a value proposition, what it means, and how it will affect your marketing initiatives. My only comment here is that you need to complete the bullet points and create those spreadsheets so you can look at your business through the lens of a customer/prospect/buyer. If you avoid putting in any of this work, you'll be missing out on some valuable information.

Target Titling

This section could go either here or in the content marketing piece, but I've decided to address it here because you can easily associate this with buyer profiles (really, they are a part of the buyer profile). The goal here is to make sure you have selected all of the titles ranges that you think to apply to this buyer. If you're targeting purchasing people, you would want to make a list like:

- Director of Purchasing
- Purchasing Manager
- Purchasing Agent

That's a pretty simple display, but it can get more interesting if you include specific subsets of professionals, like engineers. There are so many types of engineers you'll make your head spin trying to figure them all out. I want to be as specific as possible here, so that when I advertise to them, I know exactly what type of people I'm going after. This also helps if you have another employee who can set up the campaigns for you, or if you use an agency to manage your online spend.

My firm belief is that LinkedIn has the best ability to target specific titles, and you can use their advertising platform to figure out what your title targeting should look like. A large amount of information is available on their system whether or not you put any money into the advertising platform.

Applying a Code Structure to the Buyer Profile

The code for the buyer profile contains a lot of information, and when you code a buyer profile you are coding everything above it in the food chain. When you select a market, a product, and title them both, you are giving that information to the buyer profile. For a buyer profile, you almost wholly contain the information of everything above it in the food chain. This isn't to say that you have to apply all of those to the profile, because they aren't always dependent on the items above them, but you generally consider all of those items when you create the profile. A purchasing agent for a particular product may fall into the same category as another purchasing agent and have a different number (on the profile level) that applies to the same code numbers applied to the market and other portions of the system.

For buyer profiles I recode them every time I need to create a new one, per title, per market, basically anytime something changes within the profile I create a new profile code, and this is because the profile is the most important component of the buyer-based program, other than the value propositions. Because you will have a lot of coded buyer profiles, many of them will contain many similarities. Usually when I get deep into the system creation of something like this I copy and reuse a lot of what I already have done, and change it around based on whatever criteria caused me to change the profile code.

The Real Importance of the Buyer Profile

This is the endgame component of this buyer-based system—of this entire book, actually—and the time you spend here will pay dividends. Understanding buyer profiles and how each current customer, prospect, or potential interacts with your messaging, products, and services, is necessary to understanding how to grow your business. Should you send a mass email to CEOs? Probably not. Could that mass email be sent out to salespeople? Sure, they get stuff like that every day. The idea that people will buy your product just because it's there is an old-fashioned one: build it and they will come. Nope. That's not how things work. Even if you create it first, it won't take very long for other people to copy your work. Equipped with the knowledge of buying pattern per profile, preferred messaging channel, interest groups, hesitations, and all of the other things listed above will better prepare you and your sales team with a hard-hitting message.

Chapter 11
VALUE PROPOSITIONS

Value Propositions: Crafting the Message

What's in it for me? This question needs to be the most fundamental question you ask yourself from the perspective of a prospect or customer. It needs to define your marketing strategies, and I find it most comfortable to re-read everything that I write and repeatedly asking myself "What's in it for me?" It's not always straightforward, and you need to ask that question as you think about every stakeholder in that organization. Purchasing is going to ask about price changes, and engineers are going to need to understand how your product interacts with their processes or products, so on and so forth. When you introduce or change a product or service, you need to be equipped to answer this fundamental question for every stakeholder. Put simply, your value proposition needs to answer the question.

In this section, I'll talk about value propositions as a whole, but the goal is to create the final value proposition: the one that rolls up your company, your product, the market being targeted, and the buyer profile(s) you've selected to target.

Many Ways to Approach the Problem

Many systems exist that try to solve the issue of having a standardized approach to creating value propositions. Some systems follow a standard structure like "For, Who, We, Is, What" and variations of that. Suggestions abound that value propositions should follow a major brand and be a line or less—and these approaches work very well for many different companies. I like to pursue a slightly different path. I want to figure out what will work for me. Do you have a ton of varied products that serve a large number of industries? A mainline value proposition that is minimal might be a much better idea. Are you selling software as a service that fulfills one role? A little bit longer with some bullets might be better.

My suggestion is to look at how great companies do it first and find a model that puts you somewhere in between five sentences and four words. A value proposition, in my opinion, should never be a paragraph, and if you do end up using more than a healthy amount of text, the reader should be able to read and understand what it's all about in less than five seconds without thinking.

I had a pretty talented guy once tell me, while I was explaining what one of our market sizes was, "That's nice but what's your value proposition going to be?" My response was a little embarrassing, and I replied that I wasn't quite sure. Although he didn't state this explicitly, the gist of the following conversation was that if we didn't have a value proposition for the market, there was no point in wasting our time sizing it out. I could argue that unless we size the market, we don't know if we should spend the time on the value prop, but I think that's just chicken-and- egg–type stuff. I now try my best to create a value proposition before I size the market.

Purpose of the Value Proposition

A value proposition, for most purposes, is a short, clear, and concise message that explains the value and answers the question "What's in it for me?" This message does not have any specific word limit within reason, it can contain an ordered or unordered list, or it can be five words. No clear definition exists, and that's because no product, service, buyer, or market is precisely the same as another. Your benefits won't always align with a buyer, and your products may provide more, less, or different values to different markets. The value proposition is a statement of fact and value, and it needs to be understood the minute a potential customer reads it.

The value proposition is not a simple statement that proves or provides no value. It is not "XYZ hair products are the best" or "Our shipping is the fastest in the world." Those statements are not provable as true, and when you make a statement like that people tend not to believe it.

Creating an Outline

If this is your first prop, you need to create an outline of what they are going to look like. Figuring that out now and getting a buy-in from various stakeholders around the company (such as the CEO) will make creating all of the other value props down the line much more manageable.

I generally make all mainline (whole company or entire vertical) value propositions the same way now: a short tag line, followed by a sentence. My product and buyer profile value propositions are generally a tag line with two sentences or a tagline with a few short bullets. They need to be easily read and digested in any medium, from PowerPoint presentations to handouts, all the way to your website. This format generally seems to work the best for me.

. . .

Example:

Short Benefit Statement Title
  Supporting statement, one sentence

Full Sentence Value Proposition
  Two or three sentences supporting the statement to the value proposition, explaining benefit/features

Creating an Impactful Statement

I like to employ a system to create a repeatable set of steps that get me to the Promised Land. In the case of a company-wide or market-specific value proposition, you can use sweeping statements that reflect your core values, your mission statement, or your company vision. You can also create an abstract statement like Nike's "Just Do It." Apple doesn't serve any particular market (demographics and income play a much more significant role there, but in B2B that's not the same level of concern). The value propositions for their products are nonetheless useful examples of what you can use as a model.

iPhone Xs: "Largest Super Retina display. Fastest Performance with A12 Bionic. Most secure facial authentication with Face ID. Breakthrough dual cameras with depth control."

This is about as simple as you can get. If you go to the Apple website, you'll see it's littered with short and impactful statements like this. It's important to note that all of their value propositions are clear, understandable, eye-catching, and follow a pattern. They don't reinvent the wheel every time they decide to write a new statement. They stick to the same process.

When creating the statement, I start by answering a few questions, most of which you have already explained in the buyer profile and product definition sections.

1. What is the product or service
2. What is the benefit of using this product or service
3. What is unique about this product or service
4. What's in it for me? (from the customer perspective)

You can then use your selected format to answer these questions. Let's use an example:

1. Product A charges batteries for phones, computer equipment, and entertainment devices
2. This product allows you to travel without needing to find a plug
3. Product A charges your stuff faster than anything on the market and can charge more equipment with less size (of the product)
4. (As a consumer) I get the freedom to sit where I want in an airport, I can fully charge my iPhone in under 15 minutes from dead. It's flat, so I can keep it in my carryon without taking up too much space.

So let's take these four answers and create two value propositions formatted in different ways:

- Travel freely, without the need to plug in for up to 20 hours of heavy use. Charge from empty to full in less than 10 minutes on an iPhone X.
- A charger for any USB-C device with the capability to fully charge a MacBook Pro in less than 30 minutes.

- Travel freely without the need to look for power
- A huge extended battery capable of charging an iPhone X over ten times
- Flat, can fit in a travel bag without adding weight or bulk

You get the idea here. The creation of a value proposition can take on many forms. You need to decide what form yours will take before you go about creating them. You can also try out a few different ways to display and see which format you like better for your first one.

From the perspective of a B2B sale of a foam pad used in manufacturing:

1. What is the product or service
2. What is the benefit of using this product or service
3. What is unique about this product or service
4. What's in it for me? (from the customer perspective)

Examples:

1. The high-quality, durable foam that can be pre-cut or shaped to suit
2. This takes away manufacturing steps and is additive to any additional manufacturing or packaging process
3. This product is non-order absorbing and holds shape under stress
4. I can get my foam shaped specially for my need, reducing scrap at my site

So a value proposition for the product might look like:

- High Quality. Durable. Custom Fitted and Formed. Long Lasting Shape Retention

Or

- High-quality foam delivered in finished form—at lightning speed
- Long lasting form and function
- Non-odor absorbing
- Patented formulation adds to your process
- Reduce scrap at your site with our reliable custom manufacturing

Just as important as the structure of the proposition, the tone and direction you take with what you write can be challenging to grasp. Bauer, the hockey equipment company, does a fantastic job of writing the perfect value proposition. You can take a quick scroll over their site and be left with an impression that you'll be better if you use their equipment.

"So Light, It Feels Like Nothing"

"Fly through defenders and keep goalies guessing with the Vapor 1X LITE stick"

Value propositions do a lot, and it tells you what you will be doing, rather than talking about how their company designed a new stick that offers a bunch of features. They are talking about the benefit. You instantly recognize the advantage of using their stick. You know its light, and the supporting statement makes you feel something.

Instead of writing about what you or your company have done or will do for someone, you should try to write in an action oriented way. Instead of a statement like "We keep our customers' processes in mind to save them time," try something like "Process improvements save 35% more time" or "Extend your team with experts in processes." I'm not the Bauer writer, but I wish I could meet the person because it's quite an achievement to hit the nail on the head so many times.

The Final Value Proposition (Buyer Profile)

The above examples illustrate the process for a product, but the process is the same for a buyer (profile). Later in this book I take you through my process at each level to market this book, so you'll have plenty of examples there. Keep in mind that this process is repeated along every stage of identification. The buyer profile happens to be where the final value proposition is created. You will use all of them in different ways. A website might start with the company's value proposition, and if you split up your content by the market you serve, each of those markets will have a value prop. Likewise, each product will also contain a value proposition, so on and so forth. They are all used for something, and you'll always need them.

Catch Their Eye

The value proposition needs to be in a format that applies everywhere and looks good. Catching the eye and drawing people to your message is almost as important as that message itself. This is part of the reason I like to use a tagline followed by some text. Concerning my Apple comments above, their tagline is usually a product name, and that can work in many cases. I believe it works better there because they're selling a product to a consumer, one that is most likely already well aware of their brand value. In most cases, the people involved in B2B transactions don't know exactly who you are and what you're about.

I believe, wholeheartedly, that either of the above examples is the best type of formats to use. They are clear, and they can both be read and understood in a matter of seconds. Keep it short, but remember to maintain enough information, so the people reading it know exactly what makes you different and what it is that you do.

Upsell Yourself with Your Proposition

A targeted value proposition doesn't have to stop at the buyer and the product, and I always like to include a point about something that the whole company does well. If you work on a razor-blade model (sell or give away equipment and charge for the consumable), you can tout the efficiency of the stuff that you sell or the unmatched service. An extraordinary opportunity is presented each time you get in front of a customer, either physically or digitally. Take the chance to put your best foot forward, and that doesn't always mean limiting yourself to a particular set of bullet points. Take the entire list, all the essential features, the buyer hesitations, the company mission statement, and create a bunch of props and test them.

Testing Your Prop on the Web and with Customers

I've got a whole chapter on A/B testing in the context of buyer, but I want to touch on it here briefly, as the value propositions you use will be the primary thing that you test. Also worth noting at this point is that you will be writing many value propositions. Get good at it because your testing will show you how bad you are.

The code system is the basis for testing your value prop, and when you advertise online, you can use URL-based tracking or entry/exit points to determine if a primary message will resonate with your intended audience. Testing the prop on the Internet can also be aided by software like VWO or Google Optimize, which you can use to serve different messages to visitors based on any number of criteria. I like to use this type of testing in conjunction with live feedback. Test one message in one particular meeting, and test another in another meeting. It seems simple, but it requires many moving parts to work together. Trade shows are a great place to check messages; every time I speak to someone, I test out a message and gauge the reaction. I also believe the more you vary your message and get asked questions the more you'll start to see a common theme to the problems and then be able to refine the message. I refer to a specific testing program in the A/B testing chapter of this book.

Applying a Code to the Value Proposition

As part of the testing process, and like everything else in this system, you will need to attach a code to the value proposition. The point of this system will be made clear in the code system and tracking chapter. For now, we'll attach a code to each value prop. I use VP-1,

VP-2, and the like for my system; that way I can connect similar value props to different markets or buyers if the need arises. I don't tend to reuse the props outside of their intended target, but it's important to track them as a part of your campaign.

For the sake of reiterating an important point, if you're going to track the effectiveness of your value propositions, you will need to complete the entire code structure for this program. If you skip some of the code portions, you may not get any useful data, and it would be skewed because you won't be tracking every facet of engagement.

Never Perfect but Always Perfected

Whatever you do here, even if your exec team pooh-poohs everything that you come up with, keep trying. It's hard to get help when creating these things because everyone will try to throw the kitchen sink at a one-sentence value proposition. The good news for you is that because you have all of the supporting documentation complete (everything leading up to this point) you can make a solid case. You also will have the benefit of A/B testing and can get some buy-in to the process because you will be testing these things the whole time. If you can't come up with a winning proposition, you'll let your audience do the work for you.

Chapter 12
CODE SYSTEM

Code System and Tracking

Not everything can be tracked no matter how hard you try, and it's nearly impossible to get reliable metrics from anything distributed via print. Even online tracking becomes difficult if you are involving the services of a variety of consulting firms and try to make sense of their bloated, self-important metrics provided monthly. There is a way around much of this, though I won't lie because from what I can tell there's no way to monitor magazine ads and the like systematically.

In this chapter, I'm going to outline and describe how I attach codes to everything that I do so I can classify my actions, our products, and everything else that might have data attached to it. This system might not work out of the box for everyone, but I've used it over and over again. With just a little modification it seems to have worked everywhere that I have tried it.

Create Standard Letter and Number Structure

I like to use the first two or three letters of any section along with an arbitrary ordered number. I'll give you an example list of the code structure I use:

1. Market: M
2. Customer Boxing: CB
3. Competitor: CO
4. Competitor Product: COP
5. Brand: B
6. Our Product/Service: PRO
7. Buyer Profile: BUY
8. Value Proposition: VP

I always keep these in order of the list, which can be changed to suit your needs, but if you use them out of order, you won't be able to keep a regular system of tracking.

How to Use It

Using this structure is pretty simple, and just like everything else in life you have to use it and apply your methodology. If you create the system and refuse to use it yourself, you'll get no benefit. My real-world primary use for the system is to track collateral, understand messaging, create content, provide briefs, and track clicks on a website.

For everything I create I use the code structure to label it, and if you have very wide market viability with tons of buyer profiles you'll probably need a spreadsheet to remember all of it. I usually create one of these even if I think I won't have any problem recognizing it.

As an example, if I create a PowerPoint that has a specific message—for example, I'm selling my widget to an auto manufacturer and my meeting is with their R&D people—the thing might be labeled like "M-1 PRO-3 BUY-15." If I address a specific competitor product in my presentation I might do "M-1 COP-1 PRO-3 BUY-15." You can separate these values with whatever separator you want. I just used a space here, so it's easy to read. I also stay within the order of my list, so that I know that the breakdown goes Market, Customer Box, Competitor, Competitor Product, Product, and Buyer. You can change this order to whatever you like, but it's imperative to keep that structure so that you always know what you're looking at. Another thing to remember: The Market code is the combination of all available players within the SIC/NAICS subindustries that you've combined to form this vertical.

I like to reset myself every other month, and I keep

a spreadsheet with different sheets for each market (M).

The first sheet is where I keep my definitions. For example, Medical Devices = M-1. I roll this sheet over monthly, and in each market sheet, I keep a rollover of the previous month's data (and this is rolling: January gets added to February, and then I put into this column on the March sheet).

If you need to do this in a software package, you can do it in Microsoft's Power BI or keep it with your information in Zoho Creator if you happen to use that software. I present the spreadsheet option because it applies universally, and once you set it up there you can scope out a digital solution because each person's needs will be different enough that one software package will seldom fully apply to everyone.

In each sheet, I select a top-line data point, and in most cases that is my buyer profile. When I implement a program, I record the program structure in code terms "M-1 PRO-3" and explain the mechanism next to the recording columns.

The first column identifies the code path, and the second column may include many rows of data, i.e., if you add A/B test data. I won't address that too much in this chapter because we cover it later in the book. For now, we'll stick to tracking specific coded projects. It should be pointed out here that if you plan on tracking a lot of information, you should come up with a way that will make sense once the sheet starts to fill out. I also like to use colors to show what's currently on and what's off.

I add a new column for each section that I am tracking from the six listed above. Some of them you might not care about, and you can discard if you don't care to track a competitor's product along with a path you can leave it out.

Note: If you plan on A/B testing all of your programs, you may want to read that chapter before you build out any of these spreadsheets. You can combine both of them to maintain just one source of data.

After you have inserted any columns necessary to track your information, you will need to create a few columns to put in your month or period-ending data. Depending on what you're tracking, these could include columns for total visits, bounce rate, form fills, entry points, or anything else you might find useful. I don't use this as a general web metrics spreadsheet; you can use Google Analytics or something else for that. This is specifically to track the programs you create through these processes. When you put all of this data in the spreadsheet, you can create a chart or graph to display the effectiveness of value props to buyers, entry points to products, and more. After I collect a month or so of data from this book and the systems I set up, I will make the information available on my website, and you can take a look at how I have it organized.

Always save the spreadsheet with a month in the file name. That way you can keep track of historical information and roll everything over at the end of the year.

Use for Web Tracking

Web tracking will be a necessary part of this process because you'll need to test the effectiveness of your message, your target criteria, and your delivery channel. I mentioned VWO (and in the content marketing chapter we talked about alternatives) in the value proposition chapter, it's super simple to use and can help you collect analytics about bounce rates and the like. In general, I find statistics like bounce rate a little annoying when they are put into the context of a whole web property; however, in the context of a program, they are instrumental. This isn't data that you'll use to make immediate decisions over a short period, but rather the data will give you the ability to make real decisions based on what actions people are taking within your property.

Your approach to web tracking will depend wholly on the other tools you use and the budget you have available to you. I discuss this more in depth in the chapter on A/B testing. In the meantime, software packages do exist that make this type of information gathering on the Internet much more natural. Google Analytics in conjunction with Google Optimize is the most cost-effective way to track codes on the Internet. I still use a spreadsheet to track everything though no matter what other tools I use. This gives you a very efficient and cost-effective way to track whatever you want. I explain this in depth in the chapter about A/B testing.

Seem Confusing?

Code systems can be confusing, and out of all chapters of the book, this one contains the highest degree of customization required. You may not use a coding system at all to keep track of things and instead opt for plain English (or another language) to record everything. I like using a code structure because it takes up less space, and when you're the one who created it the output can be much easier to read. It's a little bit like a court stenographer, they can read and write it very fast but not just anyone can read it. It has to be interpreted. You do need to track these things in most cases though; even the best software programs can't judge the effectiveness of a message in a meeting. If I want to be able to adjust my strategy quickly, I need a master source to refer to. If you sit in a series of meetings and hear the same negative feedback each time, it's a good idea to cancel programs that revolve around that message and pivot strategy. A code system helps to keep track of this type of information and makes it much more manageable.

Chapter 13
CONTENT MARKETING

Content Marketing

Content is king, and we've all listened to countless consultants and marketing leaders tell us that content marketing is the end all and be all of everything—and they're not wrong. The most critical component to this process is showing value through words. How do you deliver value in what you advertise? In content marketing, the written or spoken word needs to provide that value. Are you offering a data set that you got from a study? Are you providing a tutorial? Are you giving some piece of information for the sake of providing the information? In content marketing, the push for your product or service needs to take a back seat to giving value to the reader or viewer.

Content marketing, the content calendar, and the

actual task of writing the pieces of content become much easier if you follow a system. I have developed this system after about 15 years of trying to figure out what's next, and it's still probably not perfect yet. Even in its current state, once a system like this is rolling, you no longer need to overthink the content that you're producing. You get the benefit of reusable research, and once a buyer profile, product definition, and goal are identified, you'll notice a 300-word article is already written for you. For longer pieces, like white papers and case studies, you'll realize that they are much easier to complete, and if you happen to outsource your writing, your writer will only need the content brief, and it should significantly reduce confusion and create better results.

The first step is to select a dataset or topic to begin researching. If you work in any company like the ones that formed my career, this is not always an easy task. Many mid-size businesses are not as cut-and-dry as consumer-facing companies. Many are split into verticals and markets that function as a group of small companies all under one corporate structure (and by this, I don't mean companies that own a bunch of other companies, although their content marketing program could be run in the same way).

The data sets that I try to knock out first are the ones that are easily supported by already available information. Let's say your company sells a screw made out of a particular material. You might have information about how this new type of screw is resistant to warping, or its head is stronger, or it removes the possibility of splitting wood. Information about friction coefficients, tensile strength comparisons, or some other piece of science-based data will make any value proposition sound more intriguing, and at the same time, it will provide more value to the reader.

The second thing I do when I begin to work on a content project is to start with a buyer profile that I'm targeting with the article, blog, or case study. I want to make sure that I cover the things I believe they think are essential. I also want to address hesitations, and make sure that the tone and writing style of the piece are aligned with their demographic, education level, and aptitude. If I am writing an article meant to drive pull-through for a brand or lifestyle company, I will not go into nearly as much technical detail as if I were targeting the same type of product at the manufacturer, co-packer, or R&D lab. Many different kinds of people work at many different kinds of companies, and their interests, experience with projects, expertise, and capability can all widely vary.

The same dataset or topic can be used to target many buyers, and this can be a fantastic way to get more mileage out of your content marketing program. A simple re-write will probably not do, but the topic, research, and information can be reused in a different content piece with a different target and put on the release schedule for later on down the line. Generally, if I spend the time on a research project with the goal of producing a case study or white paper, I will use that information in pieces to create another few pieces of content—usually blog posts or articles. I, or my team, will write these blog pieces and articles from scratch so that each piece of content retains its value and it produces much better results for SEO.

Select a Buyer Profile

After you determine what it is that you're going to write about, you need to select a buyer profile for the piece. The good thing here is that you can reuse the information that you use for the content, but nevertheless you will rewrite the articles to focus on different buyer profiles. The profile characteristics between a purchasing agent and an engineer will likely be so vast that the entire tone and structure of the article will change enough that it would be considered new.

You would write the piece of content to address the buyer hesitations, ensure that your value propositions are clearly stated, and make sure that the focus of the article is around the key features of your product or service and how they impact that particular profile. This is not to say that every article that you write is a direct sales pitch to that person, but rather the tone and extra fluff is directed correctly. You would probably be well served to actively avoid spending too much time creating content that is a blatant sales pitch. Instead, provide some value to the reader.

You can present a highly technical article to just about anyone, but the inference and the additional support information should be written for someone specific, for one particular reason. For example, if a purchaser is your target, you would need to put that information in the context of cost savings or efficiencies (What's in it for them?).

The buyer profile that you target will have an enormous impact on the scope, type, and messaging of the content that you'll be creating. All kinds of content can be used to target any buyer profile; however, some may be more effective than others when conversions are the metric of importance.

Types of Content

For the purpose of continuity I'm going to offer some definitions for types of content as I see them. These definitions aren't something that you should take to the bank, but rather just an explanation of how I see them — specifically for the purpose of this book. I want to explain how I look at life when talking about what I'm working on.

Blog Post: Blog posts can vary in length, usually at least 300 words with no real upper limit. For the sake of SEO and readability, it's normally beneficial to split up very long posts (1.5K+ words) into multiple posts so you can get more mileage. A blog post, for the purposes of this program, is a snippet of information provided in an informal way. It might contain the same type of information presented in a case study or white paper, but it is generally conversational. I've found that many people mistake the term "blog post" to mean a post on the website about someone's birthday, or an inspirational message from the founder of a company to its customers. I don't think of it in this way. To me a blog post is anything that resides on your site that doesn't fall into the other categories listed here.

Case Study: A case study is the explanation of something that has already happened, generally with information to support a statement or hypothesis. A case study will always have at least one example of how a product or service has solved a problem faced by a customer or group of customers. These are usually used early in the targeting process and should try to thoroughly explain the difficulties encountered to educate readers on what the problem means for them. They eventually explain how you have helped solve or alleviate that issue for the customer. I believe that case studies last the longest, because as long as that same or a similar problem still exists, your solution for the problem probably does as well.

Technical Article: A technical article is similar to a white paper in that it addresses a specific problem and offers guidance on how to solve that problem or approach a situation. A technical article is also a lot like a blog post in that it can be shorter in length, usually between 450–750 words. Where a white paper will aim to remove any doubt as to the best approach to a situation, a technical article is just meant to address a few key points. It may not present the only way to approach a problem, but it specifically addresses a pain point and helps the reader better understand what can be done about it. I like to use technical articles as a subset of a case study or white paper. If you have a 2000-word white paper and present all of the available solutions to a problem, you can later split that into a few different technical articles to use for other purposes. Same rules apply to a case study, and you can split them up and create a few new technical articles if you don't need to show the whole case study. Splitting articles is helpful for web content because you can create better niche topics one at a time and then link them together.

White Paper: A white paper is a pretty long piece of content, generally at around 1500–2500 words. A white paper doesn't rely on historical information of actions taken and the results but instead offers information about an issue or problem. It then gives guidance on how to better understand the question, solve a problem, or approach something differently. White papers often use graphics like charts or graphs to help illustrate something of importance to the reader.

These can be used all over the funnel and have a pretty long shelf life.

Landing Page: This is a standalone page either on your website proper or on a different host. Often, when you click on an ad and see a page with a big call to action and a particular purpose, that's a landing page. This type of content can be an essential part of any marketing campaign because it lets you be a little creative in how you present your message to a specific audience. The content on a landing page can come from anywhere: your current website, a white paper, technical articles, or it can even be a duplication (text wise) of a PowerPoint presentation that you frequently give to prospects.

Presentation: Presentations are a great source of information for a post, and most presentations can be turned into a post almost directly, because if done correctly they will all contain somewhat different information. A great deal of focus should be put on ensuring that your corporate presentations are providing the right value propositions to the right people. Hopefully, if you know enough about the people you are presenting to, you know a little bit about their problem. Your presentation should address their issues head on, while proving that the value you bring to the table can't be ignored. I choose to place presentations into the types of content that we create because they're a good source of thorough thought.

Downloadable Collateral/Content: Downloadable collateral is a broad, sweeping category of content pieces. Downloadable content would include anything that your company produces and makes available online but is not in a web-based format. PDFs of presentation materials, PDFs of collateral, Word documents, sales materials, technical data sheets, or any other variety of static content is included in this category. This type of information is often overlooked as a source of information because the tendency is to create it in a web format and put it up. For most of you that won't be entirely realistic. Salespeople still need to send PDFs when asked, and the response to a question for said documents can't always be "go look at our website."

A Simple Take on SEO

Mainly for the sake of this book, I'm going to keep the SEO section pretty short, and we'll cover a few basic principles so that you know how to structure your content. You'll find a ton of "experts" out there who claim to have some secret sauce, but the search engines are smarter than they are. Just keep your content relevant, interesting, and valuable to a reader, and you'll get the hits. The more people enjoy the content, the more they will share—and the more your page will move up in ranking. Of course, you'll need to do some things correctly as far as your on-page SEO goes, but follow this principle: Don't spend your time trying to cheat the search engine. Instead, spend your time trying to provide value to the reader.

I'll go over what I've found to be some key points to pay attention to when your putting your content to work for you, if you're not familiar with SEO then just remember and learn about these critical topics and you'll do just fine. (By the way, most SEO companies are just managing Pay-Per-Click advertising; they aren't actually doing any SEO on your page, so be wary of them.)

1. Title Tag
2. Headers
3. Image Alt Tags
4. Content-Length

You can go down this Alice hole to insanity, but most people don't do any of this correctly, particularly in the B2B world. Get these few things right, and you'll be rocking and rolling without the enormous time investment or additional spend.

I also like to use my website as the end-all-be-all destination of my content. I consider my website my house where other people come to visit all of the people who live there (the people who live in the house are the content). My people leave the house to talk to people, but they're the type of people who always have the party. If you want to see them or have dinner, you'll do it at their house. I take this approach because I want all of my produced content to aid in the total aggregate of my page ranking. The most content I have that gets people to visit my site the better my site's global ranking will be. That's what I want. If you follow this book, you'll have plenty of meaty content to add to your usual rotation of blog and news postings, and as long as it's written well and provides value to the reader, you'll start to see an increase in organic rankings.

A few exceptions to this rule exist, as videos are usually better hosted somewhere else. If you take the Vimeo approach and then publish to a page, you lose the ability for those videos to be found through the platform itself (mostly because people don't usually browse Vimeo for stuff), in many cases. If you host a video on YouTube or similar service you have the chance that someone comes across your video while searching for something else. I usually host my videos on a channel in YouTube, and I can still use backlinks in the description and use that as an additional marketing channel. The backlinks you place there help you bring more visitors to your site, so don't forget to provide a meaningful description of the video. Too often people post a video and link to it from their website. If you spend the time to put something up on YouTube, make sure you spend the time to write out what it is and give a link back to the page on your website that most closely corresponds with the video. I always try my best to make sure I'm creating a post or article that goes with the video, so that I can have it on my site and provide more context to whoever is watching it. You can take two birds down with one stone.

I tend to stay away from guest posting and providing content through sites owned by other people. I've no doubt that providing such content works well for some people, but in a B2B world, you aren't likely going to get too much from a post like that. An exception to this idea is when you're dealing with a technical source of information, and you provide material because they are giving you linking rights. If you would typically consider advertising on a site or through a newsletter, and you have the opportunity to provide content, take it. If you wouldn't usually pay to advertise through that source, don't offer it as the content would probably better serve you on your site.

The slow and continual rollout of content on your site will start unevenly if you don't have much there now, but over time it will begin to increase the value of your site to search engines organically. When this starts to happen you will notice that you don't need those other sites to distribute your message anyway. You can win in all of your niches without spending any real money. That's the goal.

Tools

I cover most of the tools that I use in the A/B testing section of this book, but I figured I would include one set of tools that I find useful but doesn't have much to do with any specific test. I think it is necessary to use a tool like Hootsuite, Sendible, or AgoraPulse. These all do pretty similar things in that they help you manage and automate parts of your social media strategy. I'm not a big social media guy. I don't even have Twitter or Facebook installed on my phone. I do think I will have to change that with this book because I will need to focus on any feedback that I might get through those platforms (hopefully). When I do have to engage with social media, I have always used Hootsuite, because I am most familiar with it and don't need to learn a new system.

If you think you don't need one of these systems, give one a try. They aren't that expensive. You will see an immediate ability to react quickly to what people are saying about you, and it will look like you are always there. The chances are good that you don't have a huge social media team handling this type of thing for you, and in many B2B cases you don't need one either. You can monitor your posts and even schedule events to LinkedIn groups or your feeds. In my opinion, worth it completely.

Focus on the Targeted Buyer with Relevant Information

With all of this information, one main takeaway should be that you can't go wrong if you write with a purpose. Musing about something likely won't garner much attention unless you're Warren Buffet and you can shift a market because you're having a good/bad day. Write to another person who has a problem, address that problem, offer a solution to that problem; be a friend and provide value. Once you start to work on these materials, you'll find that you can often make subtle shifts in tone when rewriting content—and you've got an entirely new piece! Once you get into complicated A/B testing, you'll realize how necessary these little tweaks are.

Write to someone specific.

Chapter 14
CREATING CONTENT

Creating Some Content to Distribute

Generating meaningful content that provides clear value for the reader is never an easy task. You need to have information that is useful to the people who buy or use your products, and it needs to cut through the noise. Think about the last time you saw a running shoe commercial and they touted the glorious nature of their super-foam, extra-spring, super-speed running shoe. Did you believe it? Probably not. You need to provide real-world backup for any claim that you make; people are aware of advertising games because they're inundated with ads all day, every day.

My favorite type of content to produce is along the lines of a technical article, case study, or white paper. The latter two can be more challenging to complete because they might rely on some outside source or material that, of which you do not maintain direct control.

Creating a Technical Article

Technical articles can be a great place to start because they can be taken apart and rewritten in different formats to provide you with a bunch of different content pieces. Years ago, these types of articles would almost always be gated and presented in the form of a "study." I strongly prefer to not gate any content in today's marketing world; people don't like filling out forms. For a technical article or a case study, you will need to test something to provide the results of some study. Articles like this usually start with a hypothesis or an if-then statement. You need to identify some problem first.

How to Decide What to Test

For me, the best way to come up with something to test is to think about the problems that you could solve or the issues that you already say that you address. Chances are good that you might not know precisely how well you solve these problems through your service or with your product. I start with the question:

What's In it for Me (Them)?

The whole point of a technical article is to answer that question, so if you start with that question, then you're already off to the races. I like to ask myself this question from the point of view of the person with whom I am attempting to communicate. What data would be useful to see? What is the assumption that this industry has about the way something works? Do you have the ability to prove anything to a prospect or interested party?

Chances are good that if you have to prove something internally, be it a design or formula, the outside world is interested in why you made that choice. So often we get caught up in telling a feel-good story that only shows the world who or what we think they want to see—but what's in it for them?

So, come up with a hypothesis or a question:

- This new plastic is so durable it surely can sustain rigidity testing better than any other molded plastic.
- How much more abuse can this plastic take when compared to the closest competitor (by market share, not specific plastic formulation)?

You're asking a question, and you will need to perform some tests to come up with the answer. If you're selling a piece of software that removes the time someone needs to spend swapping around in tabs, you can ask customers how much time it saves. Unless you have an enormous budget, using surveys might not always be the best way to do this. Just asking the users seems to be far more effective—on the phone or in person is preferable (rely on salespeople). If you do have a large enough budget, save yourself some heartache and pay for a service that can implement the survey for you.

A blog article can focus on a much easier question like "How do I fold shirts faster?" Different types of content require different types of problems. You can figure that out for yourself though, because I now want to focus on what I believe is the hardest to start, get buy-in for, complete, and distribute.

How to Get R&D Support or Money for a Test

You need to explain not just to R&D but also to yourself why you want to commit valuable resources to prove a point. The hard part about this is that if you have no proof of success up to this point with a project like this, you'll have to convince them in another way. Think about it like this: The sole function of the people that work in a successful business is to make money for that business. In companies who make departments bill out time, this becomes even more challenging. You need to make sure you have your bases covered and your reasoning sound. It would help if you sold your plan internally to each stakeholder, and you should be able to pass the muster with yourself first.

I like to present the opportunity to the teams (R&D or otherwise) and explain what we need to convince the people that we're going to target. Software engineers, mechanical engineers, packaging engineers, and a long list of any other employee who creates solutions is likely to know exactly why their product is better. You need to convince them to write it down. The components of the buyer-based system up to this point should help you come to the table prepared to show why this information is important to a particular set of people.

How to Conduct a Test for Content-Driving Data

A few different approaches to gathering data or information can be taken, and it largely depends on what types of products you offer, how strong your customer base is, and your access to R&D teams within your organization. Here, like many of the other topics in this book, I like to rely on salespeople collecting information. If I need a specific question answered, I ask the sales staff to ask the question on their calls. I also try to keep it as simple as possible by making sure that the issues can be worked into a regular conversation—and doing so without giving them the sense that we're giving them a survey.

I also like to create surveys and attach them to our advertised content. If I have a good targeting plan and believe that I'm reaching the right audience, I usually connect a survey and see how many fills I can get. I also like to keep my surveys at five or fewer questions, and always directly related to the piece of content that we're distributing. This can be a little bit of a catch because I would generally be asking survey questions that help us prove a point or gather information about what it is that we have already written—but it is an option. I also state in a few places in this book that surveys can be hard to implement and are becoming less popular, but at the risk of sounding like a record that keeps playing in reverse, I do attach surveys to my technical articles and case studies. I'm already spending the money advertising them, so I might as well put a survey in there and see if it gets filled out.

The other way, and what I find works much better from a value provided perspective, is to have R&D test products in situations that mimic customer use. It's their job to come up with new ideas and test products; and at the very least, it's essential to create connective tissue between R&D and marketing.

How to Compile the Information

I don't usually approach this as some university study, although it does need to have some impartiality to it, because you can't provide any perceived value if you are trying to sell yourself the whole time. In some cases, your research may not return favorable results, and when you come across this series of events you need to understand that almost everything can be a favorable result. Even poor outcomes can present you with an opportunity to improve—and then tell your customers that you've improved. Always look for the potential of a silver lining.

You need to ask yourself the question again from the point of view of the customer: "What's in it for me?" Asking this question could be an opportunity to reevaluate why you have taken this product or service to market, what the strengths are, and how you can reposition yourself for favorable results. I would never advocate lying through marketing messaging, but creating an artfully crafted statement isn't nearly as bad as lying. Dishonesty doesn't create lasting customer relationships, so as long as you never cross that line you should be fine. Sometimes you just need to grab attention away from someone else with a bold statement or image.

Any time you complete a study or perform a set of actions to gather information, you have a goal in mind, and when you discover your goal is garbage, you can still have the benefit of learning something new. Take all of these failures as learning opportunities, either for you professionally, or for your product from a pitch perspective. There have been times when we've been told no, and so we adjust our strategy to increase the chances of a yes the next time we try.

When I begin to compile information from a study, I always think about the question that started the study. You must have a hypothesis, a question, or otherwise have a knowledge gap that is common among the people who you are trying to sell to. I make sure that I put any information that I can get into the context of that question. You can present the whole thing, but make sure you are telling people what the information means as a priority.

The Power of Inference

I don't mean this to be some manipulation or misrepresentation of information, but you do need to consider yourself and the time that you spend influencing other people. I don't think there has ever been a good marketer that has sincerely stuck to fact, with maybe the exception of some food products (one date, one raisin, and two walnuts). There is always an attempt to make an inference if one data point is much better than the others from a buyer perspective; we tend to drive focus to that data point. If you buy a washing machine and it has the (100% factual) longest-lasting agitator in the industry, you would want to make sure that your target customers get that message. That doesn't mean that every other component doesn't fail within the first 48 hours of use. It's a little shady, but it's also a fact. You focus on your strengths and create your marketing messaging around that strength.

You don't always have to lead a group of people to a specific solution, and you need to accurately present a problem and some data that supports an answer to that problem. A simple solution to most real issues at this point in our evolution doesn't show itself often, but you can make your solution appear to be a simple solution. After all, that's why you're in business.

What Do You Do with the Data?

For this, and at the risk of repeating myself, you need to start with a question that you are answering. If your product solves a particular set of problems, or your service identifies a specific set of inefficiencies within an organization, you need to understand what those data points are. I like to ask a few questions that seem to apply universally pretty much regardless of what it is that I'm selling:

- What problem do you solve?
- How do you explain this problem?

If what I was able to do is compile technical or specialized data concerning a problem, I will set out to first create a technical article or white paper, depending on how much information I have. I do this by explaining how the test was conducted, the types of people involved in the analysis (to establish credibility), and then I make a statement.

If the point of the test/scenario were to prove that my logistics app could cut out millions of dollars in fuel expenses for the average large delivery company, I would state something like "The average shipping company throws away $4M in fuel every year." Think about the story you've probably heard about UPS never turning left because they find it saves money to take a longer route if they can avoid right turns. If they wanted to market their routing software, that wasted fuel statement alone would probably be enough to propel it to significant value in the eyes of a potential customer. The challenge would be to prove it to consumers/businesses in a way that makes it sound real. You would need to go drive—and drive a lot—and record all of those fuel and time efficiencies. I won't get into all of the detail of how I would set up that test, but using that as an example you can see that you would primarily use the information you gathered during your test to make your initial statement valid. It's not so hard, and you need to have a good enough question to start with, something that you can prove.

Creating a Brief for a Writer

One of the good things about using a system like this is that you can explain yourself very easily to consultants and external help. Many of us have a specific goal in mind when we set out to create content; however, we aren't always very good at explaining what that goal is. I like to solve this issue by always providing a standard content brief to anyone who might be working on a project. I like this approach so much that I use it for internal purposes, even when I'm working on a piece of content for myself. I usually run through my master spreadsheet and provide a specific set of information to help me with the writing process.

What Information Do You Provide

When I compile a brief for a writer, I include everything that I would normally include for myself when writing. I explain the market with the information that I already have, without necessarily sharing all of the contact or monetary aspects of my research. I put the competitive information, product information, my company definition, the buyer profile, the value propositions, and if applicable, the brand information in the brief. I always include my value propositions, mostly because I'm curious to see what they think about them if they are new. I always make sure to tell the writer through the brief if I can move to a different value proposition if they present a better option.

Putting Together the Brief

I like to put together my briefs though Zoho creator. I have an application that I use to store information and use it like a database, I can then use it to generate these briefs very quickly. As you build and compile all of the information required for a buyer-based program, keeping it in a single place aids in the development of any content brief. When I need to generate a brief, I just click a few different option buttons and the system spits out a brief. This does require some knowledge of HTML to get it in the right spot, but if you have people who work for you, or if you have some time and light knowledge of HTML and database-building systems, I would suggest you go this route.

If you don't have access to these types of people and don't feel that this is your strength, you'll need to put in a little bit of extra work to format the information in a digestible document. When I create a brief without the aid of a system (starting a system like that is a great deal of up-front work, by the way), I use a Word document. Because most of the information that I have is in spreadsheets, it's pretty easy to cut and copy the correct fields into a document and ship it off to the writer.

The following pieces of the brief are not already done, as they aren't a direct component of this program. You will need to complete these for your brief:

Name of content: Name your article or post.

Buyer targeted: The name of your target (don't use a code here because you're giving it to a writer).

Synopsis: I always write out the general goal of the content piece so that the writer knows what I'm trying to achieve in addition to providing a little bit of background on what the piece is going to be about.

Attachments: I always include attachment references if some type of outside collateral/documentation will be needed to complete the content.

Main Takeaways: I list out in bullet format the top three things I want the reader to take away from reading the content piece. I believe this to be important because I want the writer to maintain focus on these three items.

The pieces that you will already have done, because they are a normal part of this book, are:

Company Definition

- Company name (I think you get this one).
- Company value proposition: I always include the value proposition of the company as a whole for memory's sake.

Product

- List of benefits: I list out all of the relevant benefits of the product.
- List of weaknesses: I list out only the weaknesses of the product that might affect what I am writing about or that I could be called out on later.
- List of most useful features: I list the most useful features in the context of this product or service.
- Unique Selling Points (USP): I list out all of my unique selling points.
- Value Proposition for the product: I include my product's value proposition.

Buyer Profile

Because I include the entire buyer profile, I won't rehash it here. I'll just list it out in case you're taking notes or intend to refer back to this section later.

- Primary Problem
- Secondary Problems
- Unique Selling Points
- Buyer Hesitations
- Key Features
- Key Benefits
- Value Proposition

If Necessary

I don't generally include the following in my content briefs, but I do find it necessary depending on what type of content is being written and what it's being written about. If you're talking about a branded item specifically, then you would want to include your brand assets. If you're talking about how good you are in comparison with another product or company, you would want to include that in your brief. Basically use your noggin and you'll be fine with the rest.

- Competing product analysis
- Brand assets

What you'll end up with here is a pretty complete brief, and it shouldn't take much time to put together. It can also serve to fill in gaps with your own information. If you need to create something for the brief, you can put it in with the rest of your program. I use this to find gaps in what I'm doing quite frequently.

It's also nice because following this type of procedure will keep your whole team aware of what's going on and what it is you're trying to do as a department.

Many Approaches to Creating Content

Some people are good at just sitting down with an idea and writing it, and many of them have the potential to hit it out of the park, time and time again. I am not very good at that. I need to have a plan and something to show me all of the important things that I need to keep in mind while writing. It's not very difficult for me to sit down and write, but what I end up with is usually very different from what I set out to create (which is why I need the list). I do believe that no matter what kind of writer you are, it's a good idea to structure your content in a way like this because you can track it more effectively.

Chapter 15
THE WEBINAR

Bonus: the Webinar

I wanted to include this as a way for you to reach more people in a more meaningful way. I think webinars have seen a decrease of use in professional circles, probably because it's easier to advertise on social channels. I've been a part of some excellent webinars, and I've been a part of some terrible ones. I also think it's getting harder to find people who are willing to help present from the outside. You also run the risk of giving too much information in this setting, and the chances are good that your competition is watching. Regardless, they can be valuable in many situations.

How I Create Webinar Content

Creating the content itself is an important step. You can't take a chance that the content you're providing isn't of any value to the participant. Webinar content needs to be targeted and focused. The topics of webinars can be widely varied between industries and products. A webinar for a software company might be a little simpler than a webinar for a company that creates coatings for metal. Both webinars may be fascinating to watch, but the way you go about creating either is very different. For example:

- A software company might have regular webinars focused on training for the software platform. These would be built to showcase features of the system and displayed in a way that helps the viewer, instead of selling to them. This content pretty much creates itself and can be built by customer service or account managers who already probably do this type of thing daily.
- Chemical coating people have a more difficult time, and they will need to create a technical or scientific message to deliver to the audience. This can be pre-tested with technical articles and from watching the feedback and engagement from the written

version of the content. You can then take the most relevant pieces and have your technical people talk about it. The other option is to provide some technical help to people. If you offer coatings to metal, you might talk about how different coatings are used, their chemical properties, and how they are effectively applied to the end product. Engineers are always looking for better ways to do things and new ideas, and this approach can help attract viewers.

How I Get People to Come to Webinars

I included this chapter because most of the practices described are aimed in the same direction as webinars. You could consider a webinar a piece of content in its own right, but because they're rare and involve so many moving parts, they tend to require a little bit more work than other traditional marketing campaigns.

Getting people to come to a webinar is not the only goal of the activity, as it will provide a great (hopefully) piece of content that can be used in your other marketing activities. When I get people to sign up for a webinar, I use the same approach as everything else in this book. Depending on what type of content I want deliver, I select a channel and content type. A webinar might need two or three pieces of content to draw people in as well as a syllabus and a series of follow-up content pieces.

If you're planning a webinar, you should start at the presentation creation or content creation piece, and once you have that done, you pretty much will have done everything that you would need to do to get people to watch. I like a combination of technical article and blog post to be posted in the appropriate places. If you have the ability, without spending a lot more money, a landing page is nice too.

Webinar promotion is also one of the only times I spend any money with trade publications, as the readers here are looking for specific information (or competitor information). A webinar fits this mold nicely and can get those types of people to engage with you when they wouldn't usually otherwise have direct contacts.

The Extended Value of a Webinar

Whether or not you get many attendees for your webinar, when you record it you can turn it into a distributable piece of content. You can use YouTube or your website to provide the information to people outside of the intended audience—or for those who didn't show up.

Some Commonsense Tips

If you've run more than one webinar, this whole chapter might be beneath you, but for those of you that haven't, I'd like to offer some tips that I've found helpful over the past few years.

1. Always mute participants; use the chat box to interact
2. Have two speakers, one to introduce topics and one expert
3. Have one moderator, someone checking the chat box and interacting with people; this cannot be one of the speakers
4. Practice, at least twice, a full run-through with some office staff so they can ask questions and prepare you
5. Schedule the correct amount of time for the presentation; don't cut yourself short or take too long
6. Record on at least two computers
7. Use a headset and microphone or headphones with a computer microphone (a handset phone to call in is even better)
8. Have one person host who is on a hardline Internet connection

This Type of Content Keeps on Giving

You won't always have a good reason to run a webinar, but if you can find one, it can be worth your time even if you don't have many people attend. It's a good piece of content to distribute, and the work that goes into preparing it will make your company smarter—and the result may be content that you can quickly produce based off the work that has already been completed.

Chapter 16
CONTENT DISTRIBUTION

Disseminating Your Message

The goal of this book is not about creating in-depth tutorials on how to sponsor content on LinkedIn or how to use Twitter. I could never compete with all of the well-written tutorials that exist on the Internet, and frankly, it would be a waste of space in this book. I will now say a few words about the importance of tracking mechanisms on your content, and the task of figuring out whether or not a channel is working with a particular piece of content along with my opinion of what type of material historically works well on each platform. I'm also not going to cover each available channel; by now you can probably already figure out that Facebook is not the right place to advertise gears for an automotive transmission or refrigerator desiccant. In many business-to-business settings, you are pitching some technical solution for a technical problem (yes, even if it's a gear for an automotive transmission).

I'm just going to go over a few of my must-use advertising channels. If you're interested in any of them, look for tutorials on them on Google.

LinkedIn Sponsored Content: LI sponsored content is a great way to get a case study or white paper recognized by a very targeted group of recipients.

LinkedIn Groups: Join groups on LI. Some aren't super active, and over the past few years, many once-active groups that I used to participate in have gone dark. I still find a great deal of success with active groups, and the less niche-oriented those groups are the more success I seem to have. If you're selling logistics services, join every group you can find that talks about shipping, tracking logistics, and related job fields. These groups don't charge to post content, and the interactivity there seems to be much better than on sponsored content. Again, it's about providing value to the reader. Posting something like "Buy my product because it's better" will not net you many positive results. Instead, try to post content that helps people solve an issue.

Reddit: I love Reddit, not just as an avid user but as a technical advertiser. I can target the people I want, and there are lively sub groups for everything in existence. Think of Reddit as the world's most important forum (even though it's not a forum).

Outbrain: I've used this service a few times, and if you browse the Internet you've been a victim of it, I'm sure of that. All of the paid "related content" on news sites like CNN use Outbrain to source their material. Over time I do believe this has become less effective, but it does have a purpose.

Google PPC: If you currently use a consulting firm for this, you might want to take a few online classes through Google. They're great, and you can get brought up to speed pretty quickly. If you use a tool like SEMRush, you can see what the entire landscape of keywords are, what your competitors are doing, and it pretty clearly shows you where you should spend your time and money. I never run company terms. For example, if I were Nike, I wouldn't place an ad for anything branded with Nike. I would just place the ad for "running shoes." Your organics should take care of things like 'Nike Running Shoes.' Even if you're starting with a website, I will spend my time on non-branded terms.

Programmatic: Programmatic advertising is useful in that it allows you to define target criteria and make sure your ads get in front of those people. Many ways exist to engage in programmatic advertising, and I suggest you use a tool purpose-built for this. AdRoll, Choozle, and others are all available and help you make sure you're getting to the right place. In the case of Choozle, you can import IP address lists and create display advertisements that only get shown to people browsing from that IP. Think of it like this: You have a target list of companies, you look up their office IP address, and you serve them with ads. These software systems usually access display networks, and can be quite effective for brand awareness.

Remarketing/Retargeting: This is the stuff we all fall victim to but are generally unaware of how it works. When you search for a new pair of sneakers, for the next umpteen months you see ads for sneakers. This is my favorite type of advertising because, historically, it has been the most effective for me. People who search for something are likely going to keep looking, especially in the B2B world. Use a tool for this.

Determine What Type of Content Will Work Best with a Channel

With so many available distribution channels for content, you'll need to come to grips with what type of material will be best for each. Should you spend your money with Google PPC to promote a blog post? In most cases, you should not. Would you post a product page on LinkedIn? Probably not. It's not what people are there for. You have to think about why people use a particular website or service—and then match your content type with that reason.

Here's a short list of available paid channels and what type of content I believe works best for each one:

Google PPC—Best for: Landing pages and website content

If you don't know what Google PPC is, chances are good that you need to go back to a different type of book. This is the quintessential advertising platform for the age that we live in. Everyone uses the search engine, and the tools they have give end-users just the right amount of control over who sees the ads. You'll find waste, but this should be your first stop for promoting website content or landing pages.

LinkedIn Sponsored Content—Best for: Technical articles, case studies, white papers

LinkedIn is struggling to stay focused on business professionals, and every year it seems like it's becoming a bit more like Facebook (just without as much anti-vax talk). If you're going to pay for sponsored content to a specific group of people, LinkedIn is the best way to make sure that the people in that particular industry, the demographic, and those with the job titles whose attention you hope to grab, are going to see it. All of my case studies, white papers, and technical articles will sit on LinkedIn Sponsored Content for a while.

Outbrain/Content Placement—Best for: Blog posts, case studies

Content distribution networks are all pretty much the same, and they have access to different websites.

Care should be taken with these because it will be mostly consumer-focused. That doesn't mean people who you're interested in reaching are not consumers, so this channel shouldn't be overlooked if you have some budget room.

Trade Publications—Best for: Technical articles, case studies, white papers

Not a huge fan of trade publications, and when I speak about it in this context I mean the whole package. They may have print capabilities, a website, and a newsletter. I find that most people who regularly read these things also happen to be my competition, and I question the effectiveness of their newsletter outreach. Their clickthrough metrics are also always very high in my experience. Nonetheless, they can be an avenue for attracting new customers and for maintaining top-of-mind with current customers. I believe the most effective types of content for these are technical in nature.

Reddit Sponsored Content—Best for: Case studies, website content, landing pages

I love Reddit. It's the best. Sponsoring content here is an excellent way to connect with people who happen to be looking for what you're talking about. I see a lot of direct-to-consumer things being promoted, but I also see specific products that would not be considered consumer-grade being advertised in some subs. I think that because this website is pretty high on the standards plane, it's a good idea to explore it and get comfortable.

Direct Promotional Avenues—Best for: Direct to company

These would be like Amazon's ad platform to promote your book or sponsor your product. These are highly effective to make sure that people who are ready to buy a product see yours. You usually don't get to talk a lot about your product in these scenarios, because you're just moving your search result up in search position.

YouTube—Best for: Videos

Sponsoring videos seems to be reasonably effective to get new viewers into your channel. Because of the way YouTube works, you need to be pretty niche to do that on your own, but once people start looking at your videos the platform does a good job of getting it in front of people. You can always have an influencer talk about your product, but in a B2B world, I don't know if this is so effective.

Twitter—Best for: Everything

Twitter is one of those rare instances where everything is appropriate. I regularly click on ads that go to almost every type of content. In a general sense, if you have something important to say, you put it on Twitter. If you're spending money, I believe that the same rule applies.

Facebook—Good for: Consumers

Facebook provides a nice interface for advertising

and allows access to a large variety of demographics and targeting criteria. I don't use it that much because, in my experience, it seems to work better when targeting large numbers of consumers looking for consumer-type products. Because the context of this book is business-to-business, I avoid suggesting that this should be a high priority for any of the marketing programs I mention.

The list provided here obviously isn't a list of all marketing channels, but it's a good enough list that you can get the idea of where you should be putting what type of content. The preceding statements are my opinion on what I've seen work before; however, I've also never spent much time marketing to consumers, so this is more for B2B.

What I Don't Spend My Time On

If I have to rely on someone else telling me that the advertisement is doing well, I generally take a hard pass on spending money. This includes things like newsletters that get emailed out, or trade industry web stuff. Banner ads can work very well, but I think time and money is much better spent on a network of some sort that lets you target a little bit better. Also, I'm not too fond of email. I don't particularly appreciate getting it, and I wouldn't say I like sending it. I feel like the over-abundance of email is getting out of control, I've signed up for some services and get two to three emails per day. That's insane. Maybe part of me doesn't want to be a part of that particular problem, but I think it's more about the fact that no one reads these things anymore.

I have a rule of thumb: If it's so worth it to have the marketing department send out spam emails, get off your lazy ass and write a real email to the person. It will work better, and you don't have to mess around with things like General Data Protection Regulation (GDPR).

I also don't rely completely on account-based or "programmatic" targeting software. I find that they work, and I do use them as part of my programs, but they only take care of the electronic end. Some will take your user to a particular set of pages on your website based on their browsing history (work similarly to the way PPC ads select who sees what), and others will help deliver your message to a set of people through a distribution network. These can save you loads of time, but if you're in a smaller department, you might not have the budget for them to make sense from an ROI standpoint. The point of buyer-based marketing is to do the other work, that is, all of the work that you have to do if you use one of those systems or not.

If you use a system like that (which you can with this program, and it's complimentary and not a replacement), you still need to understand what buyers you're targeting, what information you're going to deliver to them, and what to do with your current customers. They're just a small piece of the buyer-based puzzle, not the whole thing.

Why Don't I Place Ads Everywhere I Can?

Shotgun approaches can work, and in some cases, they can work very well,- particularly if your product or service applies to such a wide variety of different people and the message of value remains consistent across buyer profiles. In most B2B scenarios this happens not to be so true. If you use a shotgun approach, you will have a tough go of making sense of the information that tells you you've succeeded and failed. In the case where your message remains consistent, you can measure ROI across channels—and that is probably all the information you need. For B2B marketing targeted at specific buyers, you need to spend more time measuring message, channel, landing page, and all of the other things that you're setting up.

I also believe that shotgun approaches are lazy, comfortable, and tend to yield results that can be improved in any circumstance through a deeper understanding of what it is that you're doing. Pay attention to every detail, and if you leave it entirely in the hands of a consultant, you're more than likely wasting money and missing out on an opportunity.

Chapter 17
FAILURE AND SUCCESS

A/B Testing

Some people will tell you that A/B testing is highly scientific, with the creation of a hypothesis and then following some system to either prove or disprove that hypothesis. I rarely see people use A/B testing in any capacity, so let's keep it simple. It's an integral part of a successful marketer's repertoire and necessary for almost every buyer-based function. I change how many different things I test simultaneously depending on what it is that I'm testing and how quickly I need actionable results. If I'm testing a website that's supported by all types of different advertising platforms, I'll generally run some pretty complicated tests. If I'm testing a call-to-action strategy on product pages, I will generally keep the tests pretty simple. You won't be going down a bad path if you keep all of your tests simple. You just won't get the potential benefit that more complicated tests can provide.

Common Testing Tactics

An early A/B comparison test should be for simple things, one at a time. Either change your value proposition *or* the form location. Change the header image *or* the call-to-action title. If you change too many things, you can't tell which one is driving the impact. The first thing I do with a client or new company is to implement a simple A/B test system so they can learn the basics, and then move on to complicated tests more quickly. It can take a long time to set up a series of programs, but if you do, you'll realize that this simple test process exists and, consequently, you will learn the systems and figure out how to organize yourself. Additionally, the fewer things you're testing means the faster you'll be able to pivot to correct.

Later A/B comparison tests can be used to compare complex things one at a time. After you get the hang of running simple A/B tests, you can start to run the harder stuff, like testing ads in combination with page content and market/product focus. This is where your organizational skills will become necessary, and you'll have to have a foolproof system of tracking all the changes that you make. You'll be testing for more than one or two variations on the page, and you will be incorporating a series of changes to a broader base number of starting points.

For example, you might have four versions of ad copy for a Google pay-per-click campaign. You might also have three versions of a landing page. For the sake of this example, we'll draw out how you would set something like this up so you can see how complicated it can get if you're not paying enough attention.

1. Ad Copy 1 -> Product page on the website
2. Ad Copy 1 -> Landing page on a subdomain with body CTA
3. Ad Copy 1 -> Landing page on a subdomain with header CTA
4. Ad Copy 2 -> Product page on the website
5. Ad Copy 2 -> Landing page on a subdomain with body CTA
6. Ad Copy 2 -> Landing page on a subdomain with header CTA
7. Ad Copy 3 -> Product page on the website
8. Ad Copy 3 -> Landing page on a subdomain with body CTA
9. Ad Copy 3 -> Landing page on a subdomain with header CTA

That's just three pieces of ad copy going to three different places. You will need to track the effectiveness of nine different situations. If you have a small budget, you probably want to avoid doing anything more than 2x2, but for most systems like this you can set up more complicated tests to gather more information in less time. I generally prefer to test a few things at a time, but I also want to make sure my understanding of the output is clear. In the case shown above, I would want to see which CTA is working best across the board. I can get a good idea because this set of information will be independent of other variables and I can be sure that if the information is consistent, I will know what the difference is. Ultimately, I want to find out which combination is the most effective, or if they're all the same then I might want to shift and find another change to test. Generally, one ad copy will perform better than another, and a one-page destination and layout will work better than the others. So I would focus my money there.

If you decide to continue testing past this point, depending on the type of ad you're running, you might need to. You will start to introduce keyword changes as well as changes to the better performing sets of ads and landing spots. You could run similar sets in a 3x3x3 nature, where sets of ad copy are running on different keyword sets. You could then expand the test so that you're testing on different channels with the same target lists and CTA/landing destinations. You can go on and on and on, but the point here is that you have to track this stuff in a system so that you can continue to learn what works best for your product/service mix and your preferred marketing channels.

Developing a Foolproof Tracking System

Okay, so maybe I'm overselling this a little bit because there is no such thing as a foolproof tracking system. You can create one that will work though, and in the case of A/B testing, it might be as simple as keeping all of your records on a spreadsheet. I know that there are tons of options out there as far as software goes, and if you're good enough, you can use PowerBI or Tableau to keep track of all of this data in a much more seamless way. For the sake of this book though, if you know how to connect data sources into either of those pieces of software mentioned above, you're probably past the point of needing this explanation anyway. Most systems that you will use to enable this type of testing on the Internet will interact in a way that gives you a lot of this natively (Optimizely is purpose-built for just this).

For the sake of explaining in theory though, we'll go through creating a spreadsheet and then you can apply the same approach to any piece of software that you might enable tracking in.

First, I want to define what my top-level actor will be. These all need to operate independently of each other as a baseline, and we will monitor the changes we make that feed into them. Because I've been using ad copy in my example, we'll stick with that for our top line. You should also note that you can use almost anything as a top line because you'll be gathering data on a wide variety of different elements, and they can all be tied back to each other front to back and back to front in order to outline the method.

I would create a column on the spreadsheet for the first variable, in this case, that's ad copy, which is what I want to test first. I will put in the ad copy in each row. This means we have one column (ad copy) and nine rows (the actual ad copy). I am using nine rows because I want to track three landing pages. I will define my landing page differences in the spreadsheet. That's three versions of ad copy and three different landing pages.

The second column will be my intermediate measure, page destination. I will have three rows of the same ad copy, and next to each one I will put in my page destination name. One will be product page on website proper, and the following will be landing page with header CTA (gated content); the third will be the content with a CTA in the body of the page. I will repeat this throughout the spreadsheet.

In Google Analytics or your other analytics platform, you will need to set up and make sure that your tracking system works. Make sure you name your campaigns something that is descriptive and breaks them up properly. Don't be lazy and throw everything into the same bucket with names like Ad #1 in Campaign #1. That gets too hard to track with a quick look.

For a scenario just like this one, you can search for "setting up A/B tracking in Google Ad Manager."

On the spreadsheet, I will track through column 3, 4, and 5. Column 3 will contain the total number of page hits. Column 4 will be the total number of conversions (people who fill out a form or take another action on the page depending on what your goal is). Column 5 will be the total amount of money spent on that combination. You can then create two additional columns for quick dollar-to-conversion or dollar-to-visit numbers. I would also make sure I exclude instant bounces, and I only like to count people who stay on a page for more than 30 seconds. Once a week I do a quick update on the sheet so that I can see where I'm winning and losing.

Using an automated system will, of course, save you a ton of heartache, but if your budget doesn't allow for this (some are very expensive), you can get to the same place with a spreadsheet, so don't skip keeping track. If you want to save both money and time, but still have some level of automation, you can pull data sources right into Excel. Pulling data from analytics into Excel can be tricky, but Google it for a little bit of late night heavy reading if you're interested.

How Do A/B Tests Help with Buyer-Based Marketing

A/B testing can be used to address a whole slew of unknowns, from the effectiveness of your messaging (including value propositions) all the way to form placement on a landing page. Because the point of Buyer-Based marketing is to direct a specific message to one particular group of people, the testing process is necessary to ensure that you're as effective as possible. Without a structured approach to your content, the best effort you can make is to guess, and when you guess for this type of thing, you tend to repeat the same mistakes and take your first action as the best action. None of us are perfect, and the best way to fess up to your mistakes is to realize that you have made them before anyone else does. This is why you A/B test.

A/B testing, by natural extension, also gives you an excellent way to show ROI and have a clear way to demonstrate the value of your marketing programs. It's pretty rare in my experience for any group of people to come into an unknown situation with a new company and have an enormous impact without testing assumptions and understanding what's going on in the industry and the people who are looking for solutions to problems that they have.

What Do I Do with the Information I Get from A/B Tests

A/B tests are all used to refine a message, delivery tool, or capture device. I use every ounce of information I get from these tests and use that data to make decisions on what I talk about and how I talk about it. In terms of the Internet, these tests can be used to determine the most efficient placement of a call to action, button, or headline text, to name a few. I like to test everything. I'd rather have a smaller number of pages on my website with variation and tests applied then I would have way too many pages.

Think of the last time you got into a discussion surrounding what your main menu should display.

- Do you talk about the markets that you serve?
- Do you show links based on your products?
- Both?

The information you get from A/B testing lets you determine the answer to those questions. Like everything else in this book and the system it represents, you are likely to prove yourself wrong quite a few times. The idea here is to learn from every mistake that you make. Just because you read on a blog somewhere that huge pages full of CTAs are the best way to get someone to fill out a form doesn't mean they are correct. Different types of people have different approaches to obtaining information and different ways of interacting with companies that support their activities. A person looking for answers on Facebook is vastly different from someone searching for software code fixes on Stack Overflow, at least in the sense of professionally searching for solutions.

This information can help you identify changes in the way people interact with content as well. A few years ago the gated-content thing became very popular for everything, valuable or not. Now, you're lucky if you get someone to fill out a form. So many of us have become sensitive to the repeated bashing we get from automated drip campaigns. It's a pain in the butt. Test my theory if you think I'm wrong.

Tools

I tend to stay away from too many tools for this type of test because I don't keep my A/B testing limited to the Internet. Feedback from the sales team and customer service is just as crucial as automated data collection. They are the ones out there presenting. If you have never had to give one of your introduction presentations to a customer, do it. You'll find out how embarrassing so many of them are. I still remember the most recent presentation I gave. I even thought our PowerPoint intro was pretty good. Holy mackerel, was

I wrong! This particular presentation mentioned that our headquarters was in Buffalo, New York, no less than three times. It's an eye-opener. If you don't have access to customers for whatever reason, give it to a colleague who's not in sales. Internet tools don't solve this problem. You need to test everything that you do, each message, each presentation, each pitch. You need continuous improvement, or your business doesn't grow.

The point here is that you need to test everything. If you find a specific type of message that resonates with power on the Internet, use that same method of presentation and messaging when your salespeople are in front of the customer. If you provide a catalog, the next time you update it, make sure you are talking about the products and services that you have in the same way you have been monitoring with your tests.

I like to keep my entire toolset to three pieces of software or less (minus Excel, because you pretty much have to use that).

Excel is the one constant that, albeit manually, consolidates all of your data. If you're good enough, you can even set up data connectors and keep your sheet updated with most of the important stuff. If you get used to maintaining stuff here, you can always load it into an aggregator later, or use it to generate charts and all of that stuff.

If you're on the Internet, you can assume one piece of software that you'll use is going to be Google's suite

(Analytics, Ad Manager). I count these two, along with webmaster tools, as one piece of software because they're made to all work together toward the same goal. GA also offers content experiments (and Google Optimize) through its primary platform. I have limited experience, but at first glance, Google's suite of tools seemed a little basic to provide all the functionality required for this program.

My second go-to tool is SEM Rush/Moz. I know that's technically two different pieces of software, but they're functionally interchangeable. They each provide something a little bit different than the other, but they do the same basic thing. Not that I'm reviewing either of them right here, but my preference is for SEM Rush. It's more expensive, but it's also more extensible and in my opinion capable of providing more information on a broader variety of contexts. Moz is superior in that it is much simpler to set up. You pretty much give it access to GA once—and then you're off and running. The reports are a little easier to understand for a beginner, and it's all around much less time-consuming and doesn't require nearly as much knowledge to start. Of course, both of them offer great training when you sign up, both online and with account managers. You can't go wrong with either one.

My third tool is very much a tossup and is entirely dependent on your available budget. You could go with a program like Adobe Target that can cost upwards of

$250k (or so I hear), Optimizely can run just under Adobe, or you stick to something free like Google Optimize. I've used a few different ones, and more recent entries like VWO seem pretty interesting. You have some lower-level entries here that are free or offer free trials, and I think you might be well served to try them out first so you can get the hang of the way these things work. If you have a huge budget to burn through, I will get set up with Optimizely. Also of note, if you do choose to use one of the more expensive options that have a suite of integrated analytics, you can skip SEM Rush/Moz.

Start Simple, Keep it Simple

Simple means different things to different people. The idea that you should start simple and keep it simple means that you need to grow your knowledge and ability. Don't take on projects that live far outside your scope of comprehension, or you'll risk wasting your time and money. You will find that, over time, what becomes simple to you would have been very complicated when you started. Start simple with one or two test criteria, and you'll grow organically as you begin to ask more questions about your programs.

Chapter 18
MARKETING THIS BOOK

This Book's Marketing Plan - Step by Step

So here we go, I'm going to lay out most of these processes in the context of marketing this book. It's not lost on me that earlier I said I can't help you sell things to consumers, but I also want to illustrate how you can use this system to fit your needs. This book is the definition of selling to a consumer, however, because the point is to provide a system to sell to businesses, I think this is appropriate. Call me a hypocrite if you have to, but I think its valuable to see how you can apply some, but not all, of what I talk about to meet your needs.

I'm going to go through all of the steps that apply to this book as I see it, although some of what I have written about in this book won't apply directly — so I will skip some of it. I'm going to take you through all of my thought processes as I build the marketing plan for this book. Hopefully, this will help you identify how these ideas come to fruition over the course of a program.

I'm also in a fortunate position, when I start to come up with ways to market the book, my content is already pretty much written. I will use what I have in the book, although I will change it so that I don't directly duplicate what I have written. I also start off with some advantages, like the fact that I can build my own website and manage my own advertising campaigns. With all of that in mind, I still need to create a plan and understand my potential audience.

What I hope you take away

I hope you can learn something, most of all, discover that the foundation of this system can be applied anywhere, and in almost any scenario - you just need to put a little thought into how you will structure your approach. Not everything needs to be overcomplicated, and when presented with a challenge it's better to fail fast then it is never to notice waste.

Chapter 19

THIS BOOK - MARKET SIZING

This Book - Market Sizing

So, this market sizing is going to be a little different than you might find when you are sizing up your competition, and that's ok. I want to show you that you can apply the same principles that I discuss earlier to a wide variety of different scenarios.

For this exercise I am taking a simple approach to answer a few questions that will define my market size:

- How many marketing professionals exist in the United States?
- How many books does the average person (U.S.) buy in a year?
- How much does the average book sell for in the United States?

See how easy that is? This doesn't need to be super complicated, and you only need to apply a little bit of math. What you can't do is get caught up in the anti-you statement - like the one that says the average self-published author only makes $100 a year or whatever the stat is. Who cares? You need to focus on what you know is right and follow the trail of crumbs that leads you to the promised land.

Question 1: How many marketing professionals exist in the United States?

If I look through LinkedIn Sales Navigator, it seems like there are about 1.2M people with 'marketing' in their title. The number I get here seems like a lot, and if I look closely many people that probably don't apply here.

I searched through the Bureau of Labor Statistics. A May 2017 report states that there are 218,970 people within the category of Advertising, Promotions, and Marketing Managers. Through all of the categories listed in the BLS site, this one seems to capture most of what I would be looking for.

Question 2: How many books does the average person (U.S.) buy in a year?

Pew Research put out an interesting study on the reading habits of United States citizens - I'm not sure that I believe it, but I'll use the numbers because it seems to be a pretty well-respected study.

- The average American read a mean average

of 12 books per year (I've never met one of these people by the way)
- The typical (median) American has read four books in the past 12 months (this makes more sense)
- 74% of Americans have read at least one book in the past 12 months

Question 3: How much does the average book sell for in the United States?

This one is pretty simple, $13.95 to $17.95. I'll probably less print and royalty and say I'll sell for around whatever you paid for the book.

The Market

The research shows that I have a potential audience of 162,037 people. I am using the 218,970 number and guessing that 74% of Americans will read a book this year. I'm using the most conservative numbers I can find.

If I were to sell my book for 13.95 that would put my addressable market at $2,260,416 in book sales. That will be if every person in this field that reads one book a year buys one. That is not reality. Fortunately, for books like this the revenue is not tied only to book sales, but for the sake of this exercise, I will talk about book sales.

I'll take it one step further because that number

doesn't pass my stink test for a realistic target - I'll try to come up with my market opportunity (or potential or whatever else your bosses want to call it).

If I divide the 218,970 total available target audience by the entire U.S. population (326M), I get .000671, or .0671% (this is total vs. total, not my addressable). If I divide the total unit sales of print books in the United States ($675M) by the total population number, I get $2.07. That's two bucks for each person. I'm getting closer.

If I multiply that $2.07 by the target population (162,037), I get $335,451. I think that number is a more realistic target for my market.

I would consider this a top-down market size - I would think the addressable market to be that $2.2M figure, and my market potential (opportunity, etc.) would be the $335K.

Because I have two distinct buyer types, I'll try my best to capture the whole market with this math, but I don't want to overestimate my opportunity/potential market size. Once I learn a little bit more about the people buying my book, I can adjust my calculations and add in some more detail.

Chapter 20
THIS BOOK - COMPETITOR ANALYSIS

This Book - Competitor Analysis

I group competitor and competitor products into the same category, because I'm going 1v1 against a person and his or her book. The product is the competitor, in a sense. I'll still analyze the competitor as a whole, the website, what they are doing and all of that, but I will group it in with the product analysis (pricing and that kind of thing).

In my research I found books without support structures, and I also found web-based programs without a lot of meat and potatoes. I've also seen some pretty great software systems that provide extensive topic-based training, but I haven't really found what I'm putting out in my book. It's a little bit of a mix of support, materials, and a book. My system is also a full system, where I don't focus heavily on any one particular topic. Many books exist that talk about SEO, content marketing, or creating a brand. I don't go that in-depth to those topics because I want to present a simplistic approach that can be completed time and time again, in a short period — the intention is not to make you an expert in any particular field.

For my competitor analysis, I am altering features and benefits to be a list of strengths. Because these are books, I am choosing to look at the market in a bit of a different way. I want to make sure I capture what makes those books special to a potential reader.

This is Marketing - Seth Godin

My most direct book competitor: This is marketing by Seth Godin. I'm sure Seth would never consider me a competitor; he's quite an experienced guy and he writes very well. I consider his book the closest to mine in terms of context and goal, he describes many of the same tactical approaches that I do. He talks about being specific, creating a structure, delivering specific messages and value propositions to specific people. We're right in line.

Book Slogan

- You can't Be Seen Until You Learn to See

List of strengths

- All-around best seller
- Author is well known and respected
- Has many books that are widely accepted

List of weaknesses

- Can't really think of any

Price

- $12

Blue Ocean Shift

Book Slogan

- Proven steps to inspire confidence and seize new growth

List of strengths

- Follow-up to Blue Ocean Strategy, sold 3.6 million copies.
- Has two authors, fantastic view of marketing and globally accepted leaders in the field

List of weaknesses

- The first book was a little bit too high-level for me. It gave case studies on how people did something and didn't show me how I could do it for myself
- The synopsis seems a little bit 'best-case' to me, and doesn't account for large manufacturing companies that have difficulty shifting strategy quickly

Price

- $20

A practitioner's guide to Account-Based Marketing

Book Slogan

- Accelerating growth in strategic accounts

List of strengths

- It was written by the people who pretty much started ABM
- Has been around for awhile
- Is hugely regarded as a go-to source of information

List of weaknesses

- Is a little heavy-handed in approach

Price

- $36

The Sales Development Playbook

Book Slogan

- Build Repeatable Pipeline and Accelerate GROWTH with Inside Sales

List of benefits

- Huge following on Amazon, great reviews

List of weaknesses

- I read this one, and I can honestly say I thought it was fantastic, couldn't find any glaring weakness

Price

- $12

I'm Not lost, I Promise

I've read a lot of books, but when I started to write this one, I stopped for a while. When I think about most of the marketing books that I put down without finishing, I realize I did so because they didn't give me much information about how to do the things they were advocating. They would explain what I should do — like "you need to create Google advertisements." I felt like I was just listening to someone talk to me like they were a partner at an ad agency from the 80s. I did go back through some of my collection after I had this about half way done, just to make sure that I wasn't duplicating anyone else's ideas — I need to provide my own value to a reader. Doing this after I had already written some of my book brought a new light, in most cases they were explaining it. I just wasn't reading it correctly. I am trying to make sure with my book you don't need to actively look for the how with the what. I offer a different approach, but not one that is so revolutionary that it puts anyone out of business. My differentiator is the approach overall, and the types of cohesive programs that I run. That should be enough.

The fact that I'm up against some very impressive people is not lost on me, I just truly believe that I can provide something useful for readers. I also realize that I'm not selling an ABM (account based marketing) program, I'm going a few steps in a different direction to provide guidance on how to get to the good stuff. All of the things like market sizing and customer stratification go out of the bounds of many ABM guides.

I don't have the time to read every marketing book out there, but as I get feedback and understand my market a little bit better, I'll keep this list updated.

Chapter 21
THIS BOOK - PRODUCT DEFINITION

This book - Defining the Product

I now have to define the product, in our case, it's a simple book that outlines a marketing planning and execution system. I'll use the same structure that I was talking about earlier in the book:

- List of benefits
- List of weaknesses
- List of most useful features
- Unique Selling Points (USP)
- Value Proposition for the product as a whole

Because the book is just a book, some of what we define through buyers, customer stratification, dissemination channels to a specific profile will all be very similar to each other. I will write them out independently, but you might find drastic differences when you do this for a B2B type of product or service.

Benefits

Benefits are what the product does for a person, vertical, or system. A coffee cup handle's benefit is that it keeps your hand away from the hot cup. The benefits I talk about here will include some of the website, although I don't want to get into the website or supplemental resources I provide too much — this is about the book first.

- People with limited resources can learn how to run big-league marketing programs
- People can start to learn how to approach marketing from a strategic side
- Clearly laid out tactical action items help people answer 'how'

Weaknesses

This book probably has many weaknesses, and I'm too close to the final product to make a good determination. I don't think I can be wholly honest with myself about it, and if I could easily identify serious problems, I would have corrected them in the text. With that being said, here are some of the things that might be considered weaknesses:

- May not be in depth enough for some people
- May not be simple enough for some people
- I jump around a little bit
- The code system that I use may be difficult to grasp and even harder for some people to implement

The last one might be the most major, and people might not realize the code system is not necessary to work with this system. It only comes into play if you're interested in the minutia of everything that is happening behind the scenes. If you're a single person department you would be hard pressed to use a system like that effectively. The only reason I haven't taken it completely out of the book is because I believe the benefit outweighs the potential drawbacks.

Useful Features

I think this book itself is a useful tool, and the support provided through the website will act more like a functional workbook.

- Offers online tools and support
- Written in the form of a program from start to finish

Technically, the features of this book are that it has a cover, pages, page numbers, and a table of contents. You could consider the online tools and support features, but even that's a little bit off base. I'll count what I've counted though for the purpose of illustration.

USP

The unique selling points for this book may not be entirely unique, because while I have read a large number of marketing books, I have not read all of them, so something might be out there that I haven't seen yet. I wanted to not read any books while I started the writing process because I didn't want to be influenced, so feel free to call me out on not being unique.

- Structured with flow-charts and diagrams
- Templates to aid in the implementation of the program

You might also find people coming from the angle of RTBs — Reasons to buy. I don't like this approach as much as the USP direction, I like to start with what is unique about a product. The issue I have with RTBs is that you can end up giving the same reasons as a competitor, in my opinion its more important to focus on what's unique about your offering.

What's in it for me?

This isn't a normal part of the plan on its own, but I need to address it. This would generally occur in your head while you create the value proposition, but because I'm writing a book here, I'm going to take you through my thought process. During the ideation and writing process of this book I tried to focus on providing value for the reader. In every chapter I want to have a clear knowledge target. If I want to explain how I size a market, I needed to be able to show it to a few different people and make sure they understood how to size a market after a few reads.

When I market this book, I will focus my messaging on what you might want to get out of the book and tools. Can I deliver what you expected?

Product Value Proposition

Widening the net of account-based marketing programs

I think this single-line value proposition statement (or

slogan, like I reference competitors) helps explain what it is that I'm doing, with the foundation of the program being based on account-based marketing. I have just added in some things and taken out some things, shifting the focus on marketing programs to people who are not customers or existing accounts. We'll see how this works out.

Change It Up

My product is this book, and by extension the system that it outlines and describes. I have two distinct parts of what I offer, one is the website and the other is the book. I think they need to go hand in hand, because there is an order required that is harder to display on the web than it is in a book. I also think that reading a book is a more effective learning tool for difficult topics than a website is. If I recognize an issue with my approach, I have to be willing to alter course and change my tune. Down the road, I may consider them parts of the same component and drastically alter my methods and language. I just have to keep track of how I'm doing at the micro level.

Chapter 22

THIS BOOK - CUSTOMER BOXING

This Book - Customer Boxing

I don't have any current customers for this book, other than my very close friends and coworkers. I cannot box current customers as it stands, so I will go through an exercise explaining how I would box them, or rather how I look at the potential customer at this point in the book's life.

I will use the 4-box system to define the characteristics of the customers as I envision them; however, because this is a book and not something that I'm selling to another business, the definitions I use will not be directly applicable to some of your positions on the subject.

Opportunistic Customer

These customers will be those that purchase the book, and in the future anything else that I decide to put out in the context of the program that I might charge money for (no plans for this by the way). They will not engage with me or my website much, they won't drive any new traffic in a substantial way to my site. They will likely purchase the book and move on in their own direction until given a specific reason to purchase something else.

Core Customer

These customers will be the ones that buy everything that I have to sell, engage with me in a personal way, and help me continue to evolve my program and what it is that I offer to provide value. These are the people that help me grow as a person and as a business. They will likely tell other people about this program, engage on the website, and provide interaction through social media and other channels.

Marginal Customer

These customers, like the opportunistic customer, will purchase the book, but unlike the opportunistic customer they will not buy anything else - and will likely stay away from the additional resources provided on the website. Because the website has the potential to be another source of revenue, not having them will reduce my ability to increase my potential profitability from this type of customer (low profitability, no relationship).

Service Drain Customer

Service drain customers will be those that purchase the book, read it, return it, or otherwise complain. These customers will take the most time to serve because I will try to make it right with them. It's much harder to interact with a person who is not happy with a purchase than it is to have meaningful interaction with someone who is happy.

Although I have not laid out the customer boxing on a per-customer basis, you can see that I change the 4-box model a little bit to accommodate a change in the definition of how I will classify a customer. This system is not meant to be rigid and unforgiving, but rather a guideline that you can use to build your system following the same basic structure.

The Focus

I want to focus on core customers, but I think the business I want to do category will include opportunistic customers as well. I am grouping these two because I believe that they are still in the ideal customer mix when I'm either talking about the book as a standalone product or in combination with the website. If my product changes, say, I have a product as a website or I engage in consulting, those opportunistic customers would be business that I have to do.

I'm going to continue to think about the book itself, not other tertiary aspects of customers or products. This will let me (hopefully) prevent scope creep from stopping the effectiveness of my marketing plans.

Chapter 23

THIS BOOK - BUYER PROFILES

This Book - Buyer Profiles

In the beginning of my marketing programs for this book, I'll be targeting two distinct buyers. The first one is based on the idea that some marketers have small or non-existent teams and work in b2b companies that produce $15-200M in revenue. The second profile will be based on marketers who are in the early stage of a career but working in a larger group, or at the corporate level in a very large organization, around $1B in revenue.

I'm leaving some of the other potential profile types out because I want to keep my life simple and focus on what my gut is telling me - it also helps that I'm writing this book for these specific types of people. When I create buyer profiles, I don't write complete paragraphs - I try to keep everything to bullet points. I want to be able to take you through my thought processes as I create my bullet lists.

Profile Name: B2B Medium Company Small Team

Primary Problem

- No real organization or goal around a tactical plan
- No experienced mentorship

Keep the primary problem limited to one or two items so you can focus on answering them specifically in your value proposition or in the follow-up to that statement. The primary problems are the ones you think create the best value proposition if you can solve them. I'll take my list above and separate it into primary problems, secondary problems, and the rest.

Secondary Problems

- Not much specific technical experience
- Gets caught up in miscellaneous tasks like creating brochures
- Small team and not many resources

Secondary problems are everything that's not

included in the primary section, try to keep this list pretty short too. Prioritize, or if you think you're getting too many, but some are clearly more important than others, order them with numbers so you can track your train of thought when you wrote them down. For me, I keep this list to 3 thoughts - its short enough to manage but will give me a place to start when I'm creating content for this buyer.

Unique Selling Points

- Modular planning that works for all b2b marketing teams
- Gives guidance on how to apply the system

Unique selling points for this book directed at a specific buyer profile will likely be repeated through the two profiles that I am targeting. When you are doing this for products or services that have a wide variety of applications, these will become more specific and pointed to uniquely solve a problem or situation. In some cases, you may not even have any USPs, you'll just have to create messaging that helps deliver a different type of message.

Buyer Hesitations

- Book is self-published
- Author is an unknown

My buyer hesitations are going to be a little different for this book then they would be for most business to business situations; however, you'll see a theme there. I didn't do it on purpose to prove some point, but like most of these lists you'll see some common connector between the hesitations. Some might all revolve around price, others trustworthiness, and in the case of this book most of them revolve around the book being an unknown and self-published. It's a trust thing between you and me. I don't shy away from that though, I address it a lot throughout the book, on the website, everywhere. I'm not ashamed of it, in fact it's the basis of what I'm doing here. It's a conscious decision and I make sure that people know it's a conscious decision.

Key Features

- Layout for a strategic plan
- Layout for a tactical action plan
- Clear instruction for many marketing practices along with a common-sense approach to how you do it.

Key Benefits

- You can now run structured programs to increase revenue
- You will be equipped to answer questions in the context of this marketing program
- You will know both the how and the why of implementing account-based programs

The benefits on the buyer profile are sometimes taken directly from the product benefits, and they don't always change between buyer profiles. That's ok, and it will save you some time if you have some very strong benefits that apply to large groups of people. In the case of this book, I don't think the benefits are the same to each group - but they are taken directly from the product. The product benefits are all of the benefits associated with the product, when put into the buyer profile they are the ones that specifically address that buyer. I keep this list short because I will be basing the value proposition on the benefits more than anything else.

Value Proposition

1. A structured system based approach to make your marketing better
2. A complete marketing program that takes you from newbie to veteran in no-time

Profile Name: B2B Large Company Large Team

This one is going to be 50/50. I am basing my assumption on my experience in what I would consider strange but common large corporate environments. There is no lack of effort by any means, and the plan is usually very sound; however, there is no real clear guidance in the form of an instruction manual on how to be successful. This is also the risk, if someone were to put their neck out like this in a large environment, they would likely be proven wrong and let go - doesn't matter how smart you are because at that level you can dictate a flawless policy but it would be impossible to micro-manage what everyone is doing.

The other side of this is an organization that is so standard and efficient that this book would never apply. I truly believe that very large organizations are split pretty evenly along these two very different lines, and I myself have never witnessed anything in-between. My buyer profile for this section will focus on the former described person, the person who is in an organization that gives them a large amount of control and may not be paying attention to what they are doing on a daily basis - this book is written so that you can actually do something productive.

Everything you read in this chapter below this line will assume you are a part of a large organization that does not have any type of real solid pre-built template structure in place. I would also like to add that this is not usually a bad thing, as it can empower people to create good solutions to challenging problems.

Primary Problem

- No clear guideline on how to complete a task. Nothing is standardized.

The primary problem here is entirely focused on those people that know they need to size a market or they know they need to develop a plan to create and disseminate content - but they aren't quite sure how to do it themselves, or they aren't quite sure how to tell if a consultant is full of baloney.

Secondary Problems

- Not much specific technical experience, reliance on consultants
- Many generalized resources, poor structural guidance

I've seen this happen a lot in large organizations, where a corporate layer dictates best practices, but may not know exactly how to implement those practices. This may not happen in a place like Pepsi or Nike, where brand management has clear instructions for marketing. But in large industrial companies, or conglomerates, the business units may struggle to find footing.

Unique Selling Points

- A standardized system to create repeatable and explainable results within a marketing department
- Support by templates that may help marketing departments of all sizes

Buyer Hesitations

- Unknown author
- Self-published book
- They may believe their system is better, even if it's not written down

Key Features

- Structured approach with clear guidelines
- How and why logistical approach supported by diagrams and charts

Key Benefits

- You can help build upon best practices
- You will be equipped to answer questions in the context of this marketing program
- You will know both the how and the why of implementing account-based programs

Value Proposition

- Learn how to implement a systematic approach to complex marketing challenges

How Effective?

I don't know, I'll have to test these regularly. An easy way to tell if these are working or not is to check the website. It will be the first thing you see. I will keep my blog updated with any changes that I make to these propositions and their effect on my marketing - but I think these are good enough for how. I also went with simple one-liners, and I may decide to go with a different format later, but I think I can list out the benefits and features elsewhere on the site.

Because the book is a book, and I will have to write something on the cover, I'll use something closer to:

- A systematic approach to solve complex marketing challenges

Or

- Widening the Net of Account-Based Marketing

Keeping a Focus

I will remain focused, as much as I can, on these two buyer profiles. When I expand my messaging and marketing reach, I will do so with these two types of people in mind. As I start to sell this book and people start to use the accompanying resources, I will make sure to monitor what type of people find this material useful. If I need to pivot my target buyer profiles to something different, I will wait until I have a reasonable amount of information gathered.

Chapter 24
THIS BOOK - CONTENT MARKETING

This Book - Content Marketing

The content marketing for this book is going to be pretty easy, because I plan on just using portions of the book to fill out a blog and create content that I can distribute. I won't take you through the process of how I get data or provide value, because you're reading what I believe gives value - this book.

I will take you through how I am going to select the content that I am going to use for my marketing systems. I like to post articles between 450-600 words, which if I took straight text would be 3 or 4 pieces of content per chapter. I'm not going to take text directly from the book though, I'm going to take themes and rewrite them, so they are the right size and useful as refreshers as well as standalone pieces of information.

I'll also put some context around them that is targeted at a specific buyer.

The types of content that I will be putting out there:

Blog posts: These will be pretty easy; I will take small sections of this book, specifically the ones that ask you to grab something from the website and rewrite to create a new blog post. I will distribute these through LinkedIn, LinkedIn groups, Reddit, and some Q&A websites. These blog posts will be my primary source of free website traffic. These will also allow me to refine my focus with SEO and monitor effective language and channels.

Case Studies: This one I suppose won't technically be a case study, but I want to keep providing relevant information concerning how my activities with the book are succeeding or failing. Early on in my career I was always interested in how other people were doing with their ad campaigns, and it was always hard, and still is today, to find real information on how people are doing. I want to make sure that I continue to update my readers with how everything is working both in my professional life and in the context of this book. I want people to follow along with my successes and failures (hopefully more of the former).

Landing Pages: I won't use landing pages in the way I have described them in this book, but I will apply the same methods of advertising as if I were. I will have a single-page website proper with a blog. The blog will be split into a few different categories and used primarily for SEO.

I have a principle that I try to follow, and I try to push this principle on other people that I work with/around. Everything has to lead back to the website, and in all available cases, the primary domain (not a subdomain or someone else's site) should remain the primary source of content and be the landing position for all advertisements.

I don't use Google Optimize for business purposes, but because I'm limited on budget compared to larger businesses, I will use it for this book to save some money.

My goal with A/B testing is to make sure that I have the right content going to the right people based on where they are coming from. My landing pages will be versions of my single product-based home page. I will use Google Optimize to make sure that what I think are the right people are going to the right version of that page.

Fewer Types, More Focus

I've decided to limit my content types to those listed above, and indeed the landing page aspect won't come much into play because of budget and time. I'm doing this because of time, money, and the other resources that are needed to expand the scope, namely other people. I also want to focus on what I believe will be most successful with my audience.

This approach is an excellent way to start your programs. Depending on what you sell, you might never write a technical article or white paper but you may have the ability to churn out case studies like it's nobody's business (like if you're in the software business). I won't make any wild claims, and I'll talk about what I talk about here, sensationalized a little but - but honest.

Content Focus

I don't want to give away my whole book for free, although I have no problem doing that, I would like to see how I do on the market first. With that in mind, I'll pick two pieces from each chapter of the book and rewrite them to be self-contained. This book is pretty long, and I don't want to take pieces wholesale for a blog post because they might not make much sense. This is an excellent tactic to use when you are pulling parts from a technical article or white paper - take a section and rewrite it for a specific audience. As an example, I will take the value proposition chapter and write two blog posts of about 400 words. One of the posts will be about creating a typical outline for value propositions and some examples of how other people are doing them. The other article will be about the essential parts of your products and the buyers you're targeting. There will be some crossover there with the articles I write about buyer profiles, but that's good because it will create some commonality and help me provide more value to blog readers.

Case studies will come a little bit later when I start to get some feedback from the people that are using the system, and my hope is that people can find problems or offer suggestions of how they are doing something better than I am. This would be made into a type of case study and also can make this program better for everyone.

Chapter 25

THIS BOOK - DISTRIBUTING THE CONTENT

This Book - Content Dissemination

For this book, I will use a combination of a few different platform. Because my budget is pretty limited in comparison to most B2B company marketing budgets, I'll take a well-structured approach. I believe this approach can be applied at scale for larger companies, and I perform the same actions for all of my marketing campaigns. I start slow and build to something that produces ROI.

I have to make sure that my tests are impactful. I have to make sure that every dollar I spend will have the potential to return something for my investment. For this reason, I'm going to leave out any hint of a shotgun approach, and I can't take the risk that people who aren't in my target demographic will click on an advertisement that I have to pay for out of my pocket.

I will do a lot of grassroots advertising that won't cost me anything but my pride - and that price is only paid if I have failed to create any value. I'll take that chance because I do genuinely believe that I have produced value. If I fail, that's all right, I'll fail fast and get back up to do something else. At least I can say that I wrote a book, right?

The Freebies

Freebies are awesome ways to get your message out without spending a dime, and they can sometimes provide more value than paid advertisements.

Favorites

Reddit: I plan to contribute to a few different marketing subreddits with some content that I hope helps people. For this, you need to be constructive and additive, because many of these people will rip you apart if you're trying to sell something. On Reddit, you need to be particularly careful to avoid the appearance of salesmanship. Keep that to their advertising platform.

LinkedIn Groups: I have seen two very different strategies on LinkedIn, and both have either failed miserably or succeeded spectacularly. I don't know what the difference is between the approaches and those successes or failures, other than I think it's pretty much a crap-shoot depending on how good the content is and whether or not groups are full of spammers at this point or not.

Method 1: People spam groups with tons of posts and may even automate the submission process - increasing the total number of people that see the messaging. I have seen this work, but not in the long run, you'll eventually make real groups clean you out.

Method 2: Breaks between posts. I join many groups, and this is a little different for the broad group term 'marketing' because there are so many groups and they are all doing the same thing. If you're selling straps that connect logging helicopters to trees, there probably aren't a ton of groups for that. Lightly related groups will still probably exist though, and it's a good way to get your message out there to people that you're not connected to. I post my articles and blog posts to both my feed and all of the groups that I belong to. You can use Hootsuite or something similar if you want to, programs like HubSpot can take care of this as well. I like using Hootsuite because it keeps everything that I'm doing from a social standpoint in one place.

What I'll Pay For

Reddit Sponsored: I'll sponsor my homepage here and do it with a value proposition for my target. Not everyone uses Reddit, but most people do - I believe that it's the last bastion of Internet that doesn't pound you with annoying advertisements, which also means that it's an excellent way to reach your audience. The targeting on this platform is far more generalized than on other sites that I like to use (namely LinkedIn) - but the people going there are looking for exactly what I'm talking about.

LinkedIn Sponsored Content: I'll pay to target specific people on LinkedIn, particularly because I do find waste here with sponsored content. I'll keep my targeting to a few key criteria:

Title: Marketing Manager, Director of Marketing

Company Size: 50+ people

Amazon's Ad Platform (Sponsorship): Funnily enough this one is, if I had to guess, going to be the most beneficial. Why might you ask? Well, because I'm selling a book.

Google PPC: I'll start very slow on Google to make sure that I'm not throwing bundles of cash into the street. This can be very hit and miss depending on what you're selling. For something like web services and consulting, I think PPC is necessary. For something like a book, I have no idea. Trusting a blog posting about someone's success with this is going to be hard for me to do, because I can't be sure if they are being honest. So later on, I'll create a blog post to let you all know how well I did on Google (I'll be honest).

My View: Facebook

I haven't posted anything on Facebook in a few years, and although I reactivated my account to look at pictures of my daughter from other people, I use it maybe once a week at best. I can still go months without using or thinking about it. Because I do believe that Facebook is a source of frustration and - oh what's the word - general dementia - I won't be doing anything there. I'm not trying to sell snake oil or get into a political argument with someone who believes vaccines are evil, so I'm going to skip it. If you use it, all the power to you, and in some cases, I'm sure it's great to grow your business (If you're into the MLM thing). It's just fundamentally not my cup of tea.

Effectiveness

I am only writing a book at this point so progress will be pretty easy to monitor. I will watch buyer profile buy-in when I can target them, and to register on the website I will require a little information about that person - like their company name, size of the company, and other elements. Although you can't always trust that people are accurate, I should be able to tell quite a bit about my marketing methods and their effectiveness. I should be able to attract visitors to register because I will answer questions to those that register for free. I won't ever charge for anything that's in this book, but I will gather information about who is using it.

AFTERWORD

Once you have a few of these programs up and running, it becomes easier and easier to slightly alter them and keep your campaigns fresh. In many cases, once you have four or more completed, the challenge of 'getting something done' becomes much easier to conquer. The first few buyer-based programs you roll out may not do very well, and they will take you a little bit of time to get going - keep at it though.

You will need to be diligent with checking the progress of your efforts, and you need to ensure that you are always staying on top of your value propositions - make sure that you continue to engage with your salespeople to get their opinions on the content you're distributing.

Afterword

ABM vs. Buyer Based Marketing

Account-based marketing focuses on treating every customer like they are their own market. Many ABM programs exist, and some are not as pointed (or successful) as the originator, but I do think there is a different way to look at life. I believe that you can capture a lot of the fanatical customer appreciation found in ABM and apply it to a niche market. If you understand your markets at a low level, and apply what you know to specific messages, targeted at specific people, you can win. Deliver good messaging to specific people and you will resonate much better. Both have their place, but I believe for small teams or for people just learning how to market, buyer-based marketing has more tangible results.

This Book

I wanted to present how I was going to market this book in the context of this program. It's not meant as a 1-for-1 comparison to what you would do in a B2B setting, but it shows that you can use this system for a wide variety of marketing programs. Although it was created for, and its focus will remain, on business to business marketing, I believe most of the pieces apply to pretty much everything. In consumer markets, the channels that you choose will be very different from the ones you want in B2B, but the rest of the system

Afterword

still works. Soon we'll see how well it works for this book.

Modular Approach

As a system-based approach (or program), this book is meant to function as a practical guideline of how marketing departments can work as a whole. Market sizing plays a direct role in defining the product or service, and budget spend in any particular area, and everything else that happens in the book. Likewise, competitor and competitor product analysis flow down into how you should define your own company, your products, your brands, and your customers. The idea is — if you follow this process again and again that you will end up with more knowledge about the markets you operate in, the products you compete against, and the people who are buying.

This all leads to creating better messaging, addressing pricing situations, understanding how to better serve customers (and when you should stop), and how to track everything that you're doing. I'm sure over time with feedback this system will evolve into something different, but I want a good starting point supported by templates and ideas that can take you to the next level of marketing. I may be proven wrong, but I think you should give it a shot - it's worked pretty well for me throughout my career.

Afterword

Final Thoughts

I hope you take the time to check out the resources available on the website, they're all free. If you have questions or feel like this book could be better - you can leave me a message on the site. I'll do my best to make sure that everyone gets what they want. My vision for this book is like that of a video game. Take it as far as you can, release it, improve it, and keep the community alive and interested through regular updates. Let me know what you think I can do to improve your experience with this material.

ABOUT THE AUTHOR

Matthew Kraska has been a marketing professional for over 15 years and has helped companies start, grow, and sell. Beginning his marketing career as a front-end web developer, he has been fortunate enough to work and learn from companies across the United States. Currently, he is the Director of Marketing for Multisorb Technologies, a business unit of the Filtration Group — A division of Madison Industries.

Matt also spent over 15 years as an air traffic controller, first in the United States Marine Corps and then as a private contractor. He spends his free time with his wife and beautiful daughter.

www.ingramcontent.com/pod-product-compliance
Lightning Source LLC
Chambersburg PA
CBHW031837170526
45157CB00001B/329